THE T-BONE RANCH

BY

BILL R. THOMAS

TO CARO - WHO HAS PUT UP WITH ME FOR
OVER FIFTY YEARS.
I'LL ALWAYS LOVE YOU.

AND TO OUR HEIRS MICHAEL, KENNETH, AND ANGELIQUE
(CHILDREN) AND
CAROLIQUE, JACQUELINE, & OLIVIA
(GRANDDAUGHTERS)

MUCH LOVE TO ALL - PAPA BEAR

INTRODUCTION

The project (book) began as a photo album. I bought an old run down piece of land in Montague County (Texas) in 1985 and have spent practically every weekend since that time cleaning it up and creating a cattle ranch - The T-Bone Ranch. (more accurately - now a game preserve).

The purpose of the photo album was to make copies for my children, Michael (a CPA), Kenneth (a Lawyer), and Angelique (a mother, doctors wife, and college graduate), Lee (son-n-law and doctor), and granddaughters, Carolina, Jacqueline, and Olivia.

I know a picture is worth a thousand words but somehow, the picture alone just didn't tell the full story of this little piece of Texas dirt. So I began writing. Enjoy.

Bill Thomas

TABLE OF CONTENTS

TABLE OF CONTENTS - Continued

CHAPTER 1

THE INITIAL PURCHASE

This is the history of the T-Bone Ranch. Enjoy it's past and dream of its future. It is land - Texas dirt, and someday may be very valuable.

<u>The Beginning</u>

In 1948, the legislature of Texas created the Texas (Veterans) Land Board (TLB) for the purpose of providing Veterans an opportunity to purchase a little piece of Texas. Basically, the T.LB. set up a mechanism whereby land owners could list parcels of land they were willing to sell to Veterans at low interest rates fixed by the T.L.B. There were dollar limits, term limits, etc. The TLB would purchase the property and resell it to the veteran.

The T.L.B. periodically prepared a listing of the properties for sale and mailed it to Veterans. Being a Veteran, I was on the mailing list. Each time I received an updated list, I selected the properties that appealed to me and spent the next few weekends driving all over the state to inspect them. I must have driven several thousands of miles.

However, the results were always the same. By the time I got there, the really good properties had been sold. The one's still available did not appeal. Most were either large lots outside of towns or a big pasture that had been chopped up into smaller parcels.

I finally gave up and started watching the want ads in the Dallas Morning News for a small ranch for sale - hopefully with owner financing. One Sunday morning in June, 1985, I spotted an ad that looked promising so I called the phone number listed. The person who answered was an elderly female realtor in Saint Jo, Texas. We made arrangements to meet at the Dairy Queen in Saint Jo that afternoon. When I hung up, I got a Texas map and found Saint Jo got dressed and drove up to Saint Jo in my Ford Ranger pickup. I had driven through this small town before on trips to Wichita Falls. I got there a little early so I ordered a cup of coffee and found a table in the corner and sat down. As folks came in, they all eyeballed me and knew I didn't belong - I even spotted a group of ranchers at a big round table and one had pointed at me. I knew I was becoming the subject of much conversation. I had not finished my coffee before the broker showed up - Mrs. Rhonda Harvil. She got a cup of coffee and we talked for a few minutes before leaving to go and inspect the ranch she was trying to sell. We got into her big Lincoln and drove to Montague then turned north for a couple of miles and then turned off the paved road and went across a cattle guard and she stopped the vehicle and said "This is it". I was sorely disappointed as I viewed the field in front of us - it was full of erosion gullies and weeds - very few trees and no water (ponds).

I told her that I was not interested in the property - period. She said, "While we are over here let me show you another small ranch that sort of fits what you described you are looking for." We got back into her Lincoln and she drove back to Montague and went south for about half a mile then turned back to the east on a gravel road. We went down that road for a couple of miles and turned off into a field on the north side of the road and went down a dirt road for about 200 yards to an old house in the edge of the woods. She described the

boundaries of the property and said I could get out and walk the property if I wanted

to - she would wait in the car. I had on boots and blue

jeans so I did as she suggested.

I walked all over the property and really had mixed

emotions after I examined it. The old shack was badly

run down and not habitable, there were several pig pens

and small buildings, a pond (nearly dried up), another

shack near the pond, the fence was in sad shape, and the

entire property was cluttered with old rusted out washing

machines, refrigerators, farm implements, cans, bottles,

etc. - in other words, it was "trashed out." However, it

had a lot of natural beauty and "possibilities."

I walked back to the car and told Mrs. Harvil that I was "mildly interested" and asked the price? She hemmed and hawed around before finally admitting that she didn't have the listing and was not even sure the place was for sale. She said she would have to check with the "Heirs" and get back with me - she explained that the owner (Tommy Larison) had died about two weeks ago and they found his body in the old shack. She said he had four kids and they were scattered from Oklahoma to Guam (son is in the Army). We drove back to Saint Jo and I got in my car and drove back to Dallas.

In about a week I got a call from Mrs. Harvil. She said the Heirs did, in fact, want to sell and told me their asking price. I countered with an offer of a lesser amount. She said she would get back with me. Then I called the Texas Veterans Land Board to see if they would make a loan on the place. They took down the information and said they would send someone by to look at the place and would get back to me.

Another week passed before I heard from the Texas Veterans Land Board - they pre-approved a loan for 30 years at 6%. A couple of days later, Mrs. Harvil called and said the Heirs accepted my offer. I gave her the loan information and she said for me to come up to the Montague Title Co. office on July 7th for the closing - which I did.

The closing went smoothly and I now owned a ranch. Now the "fun" began. I kept a "Diary" for the next six years so this early "chronology of events" is reasonably accurate. From that point forward it is based on memory, supplanted by old dated photos, invoices, check stubs, etc.

In effect, I became a "weekend" rancher and have spent nearly every weekend there since I bought it in 1985. I have put in countless hours of hard work cleaning up the place and improving it (including killing many snakes), not to mention the thousands of dollars I spent on improvements, buying additional acreage, and stuff. It has provided me much pleasure in return.

I had a hip replacement in 1990 and it lasted about 3 years - then I had to use a walker or walking stick to get around. I also had to get a helper to do anything that required lifting or carrying.

During the week I was under a lot of stress and strain trying to keep my business (a CPA firm in Dallas) a float. The ranch provided an outlet to relieve the pressure. Read on for my adventures and the history of The T-Bone Ranch.

CHAPTER 2

THE FIRST WEEKEND

After the closing I could hardly wait to get started with the plans I had (in my mind) for the ranch. The first step was to clean it up.

On the Friday after the closing I left work early and headed to the ranch in my Ford pickup. Thursday night I had packed some camping stuff, water, .22 rifle, etc. and on the way up I stopped at the grocery store in Saint Jo and got a few groceries.

I arrived at the ranch before dark and did a closer inspection of the old shack. I found an antique night stand which I kept and discovered needles everywhere.(I later found out that Mr. Larison was diabetic and apparently injected insulin). While I was rummaging around in the shack a snake crawled out and I watched it disappear into the caved in storm shelter by the front door of the shack. (it was an unusually large copperhead).

It was getting dark so I stopped gathering trash in the shack and set about preparing for my first night, on the way up I had planned to inflate the air mattress and sleep on the floor in the shack. The snake convinced me that I would be more comfortable sleeping in the bed of the pickup. So, I inflated the air mattress and unrolled the sleeping bag and fixed a place to sleep under the star's in the pickup bed.

Next, I gathered rocks (of which there were plenty) and made a fire circle, then gathered wood and built a campfire. After the fire burned down I cooked a T-bone steak over the coals and heated a can of beans. A slice of bread and a cold beer completed the meal.

It was beginning to get dark when I put the steak on the grill and the coyote serenade; which was to become a very familiar tune, got started. It seemed that coyotes were howling in every direction. At first it was sort of spooky but after awhile I got used to it and later would come to enjoy it and look forward to it each night.

After supper I sat on the tailgate of the truck, smoked a cigarette, and sipped on a cold beer and enjoyed the night sounds. I started getting sleepy so I crawled into the sleeping bag and was soon making z's.

Sometime during the night something woke me up. I lay there in the sleeping bag and listened. It was very dark (new moon) and I couldn't see a thing. Directly, I heard a noise - a crunching sort of noise - and it was close - sounded like it was coming from approximately where the campfire had been. I felt around and finally located my flash light and .22 rifle. I sat up and shined the light in the direction the noise had come from. Two fireballs appeared in the light and I aimed the rifle at them and fired.

Whomp! The bullet struck home. I slipped on my boots and slid out of the truck to investigate. What I found was a bobcat - a very large bobcat. He had been chewing on the T-bone from last night's steak.

I thought man, this is a wild place (and am I going to love it). I crawled back into my sleeping bag and slept till sun up. When I got up, I looked across the front field and saw five deer, and knew for sure I was going to love this wild place which I decided to name - The T-Bone Ranch.

CHAPTER 3

WEEKEND ROUTINE - THE FIRST YEAR

We still owned a lake house at Hide Away Lake over in East Texas (near Tyler) so I spent about half my weekends that first year at the lake house. However, I soon realized that I really enjoyed the ranch weekends much more so I put the lake house up for sale. About then the economy was in a nose dive so I ended up swapping the lake house for a Cadillac Seville, cash, and a slow note.

Meanwhile, back at the ranch the cleanup project continued. Each weekend I gathered the small trash (cans, needles, nails, wire, etc. in plastic bags) and picked up the larger trash and loaded it into the pickup and hauled it to a big ditch on the east side of the property and dumped it. The idea was to fill the ditch with the junk then have a bulldozer push dirt on the top of it. (Here it is, twenty five years later and I still throw trash in that ditch and only have it half filled - no dirt yet.

Another thing that became routine was - fixing flats. Hardly a weekend passed that I didn't have at least one flat on the pickup - sometimes more - many more. I didn't think I would ever get all the nails, screws, needles and other chunks of metal with sharp edges picked up - and still have not - not 100% - maybe 70-80%. I bought a metal detector and large magnet and cleared all the roads and part of the fields - but not all.

After that first weekend I took a wall tent up and sat up a semi permanent camp in the woods near the pond. I had to pack in water and use the woods for a bathroom - it was awfully hot in the summer so I usually couldn't get to sleep till about midnight. The tent had a floor and a mesh zip up door so I didn't worry about snakes, coons, etc. I began to thin out the snakes that first year also. I bought a .22/410 over under which I kept in the truck. The .410 was deadly on the snakes - mostly small copperheads with an occasional rattlesnake thrown in for variety and excitement. If you have never been in tall weeds and brush and heard a rattlesnake buzzing nearby, you ain't lived.

After I had picked up most of the big stuff (refrigerators, etc.) and hauled them to the ditch, I began to pick up dead tree limbs and rocks along with cans, etc. I bought a small trailer and pulled it behind the truck. I also bought a small (too small) chain saw and began trimming and cutting trees. My routine was - metal went into trash bags which were put into the pickup bed and hauled to the ditch; rocks were put into the pickup bed and hauled to a rock pile I had started down by the second shack (which I was later told had been the home of some Mexican wetbacks that worked for Mr. Larison, the decreased former owner who had raised cows, pigs, and wheat on the property). The tree limbs and any trash which would burn (i.e. plastic, cardboard, paper, boards, etc.) was loaded into the trailer and hauled to a big "burn pile" I had started in the middle of the front field. I also threw snakes, skunks, and coons I had killed in the burn pile (and buzzards were nearly always floating overhead).

CHAPTER 4

DICK AND THE BIG FIRE

On Christmas Eve of that first year, Dick Cadena, my wife's sisters' husband, wanted to see the place so we hopped into my pickup and drove up. The distance from Dallas was about 75 miles but in those days there wasn't that much traffic to fight so I could usually make the trip in about an hour and a half. (Today it takes over two hours.)

Even though I had spent many weekends picking up trash, the place still looked shoddy (grown up in weeds) and I had not torn down the old pig pens, etc. or done anything to the shack except haul off trash. The "snake pit" storm cellar was still there. I could tell that Dick wasn't too favorably impressed.

The thing that seemed to bother Dick the most was the huge pile of limbs out in the field. He inquired about them a couple of times. I explained to him that I was waiting for it to snow before I burned the pile of limbs. He wanted to burn it - now.

However, as we were getting ready to leave he noted that it was calm and the ground was damp (from a recent rain) so I said, "What the heck let her burn" and Dick lit a match to the pile. After it got to burning good (flames leaping about 10 feet up) the wind started blowing and scattered sparks to hell and back. I jumped into the truck and rushed back to the old shack and got two shovels and we started trying to put out the grass fires that were springing up on the downwind side of the brush pile.

In no time the fire was out of control and had burned right up to where the truck was parked. I motioned for

Dick to get behind the fire and I jumped into the truck and raced down the gravel road to the first house I came to. (an old couple named Shaw). I whipped into their driveway, frantically blowing the horn. The old woman stuck her head out the door and I yelled "Fire". She saw the smoke and said "My goodness - I'd better call the fire department." I yelled "Thanks", backed out, and headed back to the burning T-Bone.

When I got back to the ranch the fire was raging. The wind was blowing out of the southwest so the fire was moving down the hill and toward the big gully. Dick was between the fire and the old shack - doing what he could with a shovel to prevent it from reaching the old shack. by the time I parked and got out, we could hear a siren coming down the road from Montague.

Directly, a surplus Army 6 by 6 with water tank on it turned in the gate and drove up. They were ready to chase the leading edge of the fire but I convinced them that the gully would stop it - I suggested they put out the edges nearest the old shack to save the shack. they followed my suggestion and the "Homestead" was saved. By the time they finished around the shack and on top of the hill, the fire had burned down to the gulley and didn't jump it. (the gulley was at least 40 feet deep and about 100 feet wide).

The firefighter from the Montague volunteer fire department spent about another hour squirting water on isolated burning logs, etc. and had the fire put out. I thanked them and they left . I will be forever grateful to the Montague Volunteer Fire Department. There was nothing more that Dick and I could do so we headed back to Dallas - looking like escapees from a disaster area - sooty and dirty and smelling of smoke.

Follow Up Comments

When I got back to the ranch the next weekend I discovered the fire had not been completely extinguished. It had reignited and burned its way northward along the creek (gulley) bank and westward across the back side of the property into the middle of Truman Weed's field. Truman said the Montague boys spent most of Monday fighting the fire.

I wrote a letter to the Montague Volunteer Fire Department and thanked them again - also made a substantial contribution and continued to do so annually at their fund drives.

In hindsight, the fire was a blessing - it burned a lot of brush, weeds, etc. - the next year there was more grass - and fewer snakes.

CHAPTER 5

HISTORY OF MONTAGUE COUNTY

I have always been fascinated with history. One weekend I was browsing through the Montague County Shopper, a weekly newspaper and ad flyer, ("Shopper") and saw an ad for a book for sale - the story of Montague County, Texas. I called the phone number and this led to a visit to the home of the editor, Melvin Fenoglio. I spent several hours visiting with Melvin and, of course, purchased the book. (the book now has a place of honor in the Thomas library). If you want to dig deeper into the history of Montague County, read the book. In this chapter I will attempt to "hit the high spots.

Let me describe the Shopper before I forget. The "Shopper" is a magazine size newspaper published every

Thursday in Bowie. It is basically a want ad's publication with practically no news - except a report on the court house activity - property transfers, law suits, and divorces. I came to rely on the want ads for trades, purchases of used equipment, etc. I did not have a mail box at the ranch so I rented a P.O. Box in Saint Jo.

Prior to 1841, the land around Montague was inhabited by the Indians - principally the Comanche's, Kiowa's, and Wichita's. Buffalo roamed throughout the county which consisted of three geographies - the cross timbers, grand prairie, and lower plains. A few brave and/or foolish white men ventured into the county starting around 1850. But by 1870, the population was only 885. (Texas had won its independence in 1836 but most of the early settlement was in the southeast quadrant of Texas).

The settlement of the county didn't begin in earnest until the end of the Civil War. The early cattle drives along the Chisholm Trail came through Montague County - which became known as the "County of Trails."

The Indians were chased out by 1870. However, they continued to cross the Red River from Oklahoma and raid the early villages (many of which became ghost towns) until 1872. By 1900 the population had grown to 24,800.

Oil was discovered near Nocona in 1924. Today the economy remains dependent on agriculture and oil. However, agriculture has changed from predominately crops (cotton, grain, etc.) to predominately cattle (ranching).

Wal-Mart built one of their "Super Centers" in Bowie and ran practically all of the small merchants out of business. The local economy was terrible.

CHAPTER 6

MACHINES HELP - THE FIRST TRACTOR

It became obvious that I needed a tractor and other equipment if I was ever going to get the weeds and brush under control. I started watching the ads in the Dallas Morning News and finally spotted what I thought to be a real "Bargain." - A Ford 8N and a "Bush Hog" for $5,000. I called the phone number listed and got the information.

The owner was <u>Joe</u> <u>Burch</u> and he lived in Anna, Texas. I made arrangements to meet him at his house on Saturday morning.

I drove up the following Saturday and inspected the "bargain." Much like the ranch itself, it was not very impressive looking - but it had "possibilities." The tractor was ancient - one of the first 8-N's built (1947) and it was quite beat up, rusted out, hard to start, tires wore out, etc. etc. The "Bush Hog" turned out to be a "Covington Cutter" mower - also ancient with a rusted out deck (However, it had a recent liquid (paint) overhaul).

After some serious negotiating the "deal" became - Mr. Burch would throw in a bucket attachment, a spare battery and deliver the whole kit n kaboodle to the T-Bone Ranch for $4,000 - $2,000 down and $2,000 at delivery. I helped him load on to his big flatbed trailer and he followed me to the ranch.

When we got to the T-Bone and unloaded, I paid him but before he could get away I asked him to "show me" how the tractor and mower work. He commenced to crawfish and said he was in a hurry to get back home.

(He had some weak excuse which I have forgotten). After I threatened to stop payment on the checks if he didn't show me how to operate the tractor, he reluctantly complied. The first steps he took were (1) get a can of gasoline and pour some into the gas tank, (2) get a can of oil and pour some into the oil fill pipe, and (3) get a wrench, funnel and gallon of hydraulic oil and pour most of it in the hydraulic oil filler hole - while doing these things he was warning me to check all 3 before starting the tractor. He admitted that the tractor leaked a "little bit." Then he climbed onto the tractor and tried to start it - the battery wouldn't turn the engine over. He climbed back down and took out the battery and replaced it with the spare battery he had sold to me. While doing this he asked if I had a battery charger. I said "No."

He climbed back on the tractor and it cranked and started this time - and belched a lot of smoke. He engaged the power take off and drove out into the field and cut a swath though the weeds and drove back to me and got off. He left the tractor running and asked me to try it. I climbed aboard and cut another swath through the weeds, then drove back to where he stood. He gave me a piece of paper with a name and phone number on it - Charles Gillstrap - 817-490-9902. he said the man had a tractor business in Saint Jo and I should call him if I had any problems with the tractor. (I thought I recognized the name - but wasn't sure). He drove off and I got back on the tractor and proceeded to mow.

I mowed for about an hour and the tractor started sputtering and then quit  running. I tried to restart it but the battery was dead - also, the fuel tank was empty. I took out the battery, loaded it into my truck, and drove into Bowie. I left the battery at a Conoco station and drove to the Napa Auto parts store and purchase a gas can, some motor oil and hydraulic oil, a funnel, and a battery charger. Then I went by the Dairy Queen and ate a hamburger then went back by the Conoco station and filled the gas can and picked up the battery and headed back to the T-Bone.

When I got back to the T-Bone I found my tractor problems were not completely solved - one of the rear (big) tires was flat. I drove back to Montague to the small Shell station and grocery store and borrowed their phone directory and phone and called a couple of tire repair places before I located an independent tire repair man who would come to the ranch and fix the flat. Then

I went back to the ranch and waited till near dark before he showed up in a junky old truck. However, he had the tools to remove the wheel, then tire, and patch it up. It had a tube in it. He also put a boot in the tire to patch the hole in it. His total bill - $20 - I gave him a $10 tip.

I got tractor going again and mowed till dark. Then I shut it down and headed for my camp. However, before I left the tractor I disconnected one cable. By then I had figured that there was a short somewhere that was draining the battery and the belt on the generator was so worn and loose that it probably wasn't even "ginning."

I could go on and on about all the problems I had with that old Ford 8-N tractor but the cold brutal fact was - it was <u>completely</u> <u>worn</u> <u>out</u> and it was going to cost quite a bit of money to get it serviceable and reliable. I'm not a mechanic but any fool could figure that out - especially if he tried to "work" the old tractor for a full day. Most of the time I had to mow the high weeds in first gear - the old Ford didn't have enough power to pull your hat off.

But one thing that worked well was that old Covington cutter - it was "Heck for stout." There is no telling how many rocks and stumps I whacked with it nor how many times it got tangled in old barbed wire, etc. Other than sharpening it, adding gear oil, ad having it welded a couple of times - it just kept on cutting. Without it, I would never have gotten the T-Bone cleaned up. I finally threw it in the trash in 2002 when I bought a new Howse 6' mower. By then I was down to smooth mowing - all the rocks and most of the stumps were gone.

I ran old Ford 8-N every weekend for several months and one by one fixed many of its problems - i.e. leaky fuel line, replaced the oil plug gasket, replaced a seal in the hydraulic system, replaced the spark plugs, fixed the short (an exposed wire). I bought a shop manual from the Dallas Ford tractor dealer and became a reasonably good shade tree mechanic. I also bought additives and poured into its bowels (i.e. Marvel Oil).

However, despite all the pampering the old Ford 8-N finally really died on me - I couldn't fix it any further so I called Charlie Gillstrap and he came out one Saturday . I did know him and he remembered me. Charlie had been the manager of Ben Griffin Tractor Company, an audit client in Dallas that I had audited for several years back in the late 50's. He had married a woman from Saint Jo a few years back and moved up there and started a little business called Saint Jo Tractor Company. His company did tractor service but mostly he went all over the country buying used tractors (at auctions, from new tractor dealers, etc.) and hauling them to his used tractor lot in Saint Jo for resale. In other words, he was a modern day horse trader. (As I was soon to learn).

We visited for a while and he said that he would send his boy out next week to pick up the 8-N and haul it to his shop to check it out. I said "Ok" and he left. I piddled around for awhile and headed back to Dallas.

I didn't hear from Charlie the next week so the following Friday afternoon I went to Saint Jo Tractor before I headed to the ranch. Charlie was leading a local rancher through his lot and they had stopped by a purty good looking Allis Chalmers tractor and seemed to be dickering. Charlie saw me and yelled and told me to grab a coke and wait in his air conditioned office and he would get with me directly. So I did.

When Charlie came into the office he scratched his head, shuffled his feet and finally said "Bill, I shore hate to tell you this but your old 8-N is plumb wore out - it would take more to fix it than it is worth."

I asked him, "Charlie, what do you recommend?"

He said, "I just got back from Iowa and included in the stuff I bought is a sweet running little 9-N Ford that I think you would like - let's go take a look at it."

Like a mouse following the pied piper, I followed Charlie through the used tractors up to the Ford/Ferguson 9-N sitting at the back of the lot. It was muddy and had the usual dents and scrapes but it did start on the first try - however it was missing purty bad."

Charlie explained, "We just got through unloading it off the trailer and haven't run it through the shop to check it out yet - I can tell it's going to need new spark plugs -

but we'll check it out real good and fix anything that needs fixing."

I inquired - "How much will you trade for?"

More head scratching and foot shuffling then he reared back and said "I bought that 9-N for an ole boy up in Spanish Fort and I know he will pay me good for it. Heck, he said, your old 8-N ain't worth fixing but since it is you - I reckon I'd swap for $5,000 boot."

I retaliated with "Charlie, you're crazy as a bessy bug - were so far apart on a deal I'm wasting my time" so I got up and headed for my pickup.

He yelled "Wait up Bill - don't get mad at me - let's talk - what would you give?"

I continued to my truck and climbed up in the seat and he walked up and motioned for me to roll down the window.

He asked again "How much will you give? I though a

minute and reached over and picked up my check book and glanced at the balance - $3,100, so I said "I'd give you my tractor and $2,500."

He thought for a minute and asked "Are you still doing tax work?"

I said "Sure."

He thought a little longer and finally said "I know this is a bad deal for me but I'd make this swap -

*I'll give you the 9-N in good working order - in other words, after we run it through our shop - and you would give me:

*three years of completed tax returns.

*a financial statement on my business for my banker (a compilation in accounting lingo)

*$2,500

*A note for $1,000 which you could pay when you have the money.

I thought for a minute and replied - "If you will put better tires on the 9-N, they don't have to be new, and take $2,000 now instead of $2,500, no note for $1,000 and all other points unchanged, and deliver the tractor to my ranch, and warrant working condition of the 9-N for 90 days - I'll swap."

He said "Dad blame, you drive a hard bargain - but it's a deal" and he stuck out his  hand and we shook.

I wrote him a check for $2,000 and drove to the grocery store and picked up a few things before heading to the T-Bone.

The era of the Ford 8-N had finally come to a close.

At about this time I began to have weekend visitors. The old shack was barely habitable but I had built a couple of beds and got some used springs and mattresses, built a table and bench, added a wood burning stove, and bought a couple of five gallon water cans. I had a Coleman Gas stove for cooking and a Coleman lantern for night. Among my early guests were Hamilton Rial, Omar Lenin, Howard Freeman, William Rushing, and Michael Shahim.

Hamilton   Omar

Howard

42

They all had "you should" suggestions but were not that eager to pitch in and help - but sometimes did and I appreciated it.

Milton (my neighbor on the south side) had warned me about the deer poachers. One morning before daylight I heard a Boom! Boom! by my front gate. I jumped up and saw a spot light shining out in the field near the gate. There was a pickup and two hunters loading a deer into the truck - within 50 feet of a "No Hunting" sign I had nailed to a tree. I yelled at them - "No hunting and no trespassing on this place!!!" That was followed by another Boom! And the bullet whacked a tree limb overhead. I had a powerful 8mm Mauser in the truck so I put on my shoes and went and got it. It had a telescope sight and I loaded it and sighted at the truck. It was light enough to that I could take a bead - the poachers had already climbed into the cab so I aimed at the wall of the bed of the truck and pulled the trigger. K-Boom! - Whomp! I'm sure they felt the impact of that large bullet. They left spinning their wheel all the way. Word got out - don't trespass on the T-Bone - a wild man lives there!

By now I had mowed the front pastures a couple of times and picked up most of the big rocks and trash that I uncovered. I took some soil samples and sent them off to be analyzed.

I bought a 14 chisel plow and a disc and plowed, disc, and drug (I made a homemade drag out of railroad ties) these front pastures. After I got the results of the soil tests I began to fertilize the fields heavily and scatter Bermuda grass seed. The Bermuda grass came up and slowly but surely it started to take over and choke out the weeds - provided I kept the fields close mowed so the grass could get sunlight.

There was a hillside that was badly eroded; so I later plowed it with a breaking plow and terraced it before I planted red clover. The clover came back - year after year and brought the nitrogen level up in doing so.

The front pastures were starting to look good - but the woods and brush on the back remained.

CHAPTER 7

MEETING THE COLORFUL NEIGHBORS

I have never been an outgoing person - matter of fact I am rather shy (typical introverted shiny pants bookkeeper I suppose) so it took a while to meet the neighbors. I'm also somewhat of a traditionalist (old fashioned maybe). Where I grew up, the neighbors always came by when someone new moved into the neighborhood and the stranger didn't have to make a special effort to go meet them. I waited them out and they finally stopped by - with some time elapsing between each meeting. Here were the neighbors.

Milton

One day after I had cleaned up the place purty good and was staying in the old shack, I heard someone coming and looked out and saw an old tan Dodge sedan pull up and stop under a shade tree.

I stepped outside as he was getting out of his car. We introduced ourselves. He was few years older than me and his name was Milton. Milton grew up in and lived most of his life in Dallas. He had been in the wholesale business - supplied vending machines. He had retired about five years prior and moved to his ranch (Stone River Ranch - across the road from me on the south side).

Milton was (he died in 2000) a good man - very shy and very low key - and very frugal! (Thus the old junk car and grown up ranch).

I fixed a pot of coffee and we visited for an hour or so. He kept complimenting me on how nice my place looked. I found out the following from our visit.

He and his wife, Dorothy, lived in a house trailer off in the woods - you couldn't see it from the road. His ranch was nearly 1,000 acres. His wife had inherited the ranch - she was a Carminati. When they first moved out there he had bought a couple of quarter horse mares and a stud. Since then they had reproduced and he thought there were about twenty "wild" horses on his place.

His big hang ups were (a) poachers (b) owls, and (c) rats and mice.

He gave me his phone number along with the numbers for the local game warden (Jim) and a local rancher who he recommended if I ever needed to buy cows or horses (David). Milton claimed that hunters were always slipping on to his property and shooting his deer. He said they had been on my place too - he had seen them. I told him I had posted my place and that pleased him.

Dorothy liked cats but they could never keep one long - the owls got them. This too he claimed to have seen.

And finally, he taught me how to trap rats and mice. He said "use acorns for bait." I tried it and it worked.

He and Dorothy only had one child - a son who lived in Wichita Falls - and three grandchildren.

Milton kept his gate double locked so I never did get over to their house trailer to visit them. However, on numerous occasions when I would be on the tractor and near the road he would always stop if he saw me and I would drive up to his car and we would "visit." He would drive down to his mail box by the front gate every day; so if I needed to visit with him I would watch for his approach and drive up to catch him.

I met his wife, Dorothy, at one of our roadside visits. She was from one of the old pioneer families in Montague County. The Stone River Ranch had been in her family for 5 or 6 generations.

Truman

Truman's ranch bordered the T-Bone on the northwest corner (near my pond). I was down at the pond one day and heard a tractor running - I walked to the fence corner to see who it was and he was mowing his pasture. He saw me and drove over and stopped and got down and walked over - we introduced ourselves and visited for a few minutes. He wanted to get back to mowing but promised to come over the next day for a longer visit. I invited him for dinner.   I liked him right off and the feeling seemed to be mutual.

The next day (a Sunday) I heard someone coming and looked out and saw a battered old Chevy pickup coming down the road toward the old shack.   He got out and I met him and invited him in.

With my very limited facilities I had prepared a purty good meal as follows:

*Beef stew
*Green beans
*Fried corn cakes
*Peach cobbler

I had prepared most of this in a dutch oven over a wood fire outside.   Ole Truman ate like he was starved. He bragged on that meal for the rest of his life (which ended in 2002).

Truman had lived around Montague all his life.   He had been widowed about ten years and lived alone in an old run down stone house on his ranch. The road in front of his place is named Weed Road. He had spent most of his life in the "oil patch" (as a roughneck).

He told me a lot about the history of the area and the people. One of his sons lived in Saint Jo.

I remember that in one of our visits our conversation got around to cattle ranching and I asked "Truman, how do you get into the cattle ranching business?" He grinned and said "First, you inherit a good ranch." (How true that proved - you couldn't pay debt service on pasture land and make any money raising cattle).

Jim Ed

Jim Ed's ranch joined the T-Bone on the east boundary. It was one of the best looking ranches in the area. The biggest attraction of his place was a battery of big tanks painted silver with a blue band around them and several pump jacks that operated 24/7.

He lived in Bowie but ran cattle on his place and came out every day in his new red Ford pickup. I waved at him several times as he drove past but he never offered to stop - or even slow down. Sometimes he waved back - sometimes he didn't.

I decided "the heck with him."

He finally showed up one cold rainy night. His prize bull had gotten out and he was pretty sure it had gotten through the fence adjoining my property. I told him we could go look for the bull. We got into his truck which was a 4x4 and slipped and slid down to the creek - and found his bull in a little patch of woods - trying to stay dry, and warm.

We agreed that the bull wasn't going anywhere so he said he would come back after daylight and bring his trailer. I told him I'd help him get the bull loaded.

He came back early the next morning and had a bucket of range cubes in his truck. With that "carrot", he led the bull right into the trailer and then drove off - without saying a darn word.

He never came back but always waved whenever he saw me. Sometimes I wave back - sometimes I don't.

Unknown Owner From Abilene

I never met the owner of the ranch which joins the north boundary. It is mostly wooded and the creek which runs through the T-Bone continues through it. It is really rough and rugged country and most of the deer and wild turkey live on it. They come on to the T-Bone for food.

According to Truman, most of the country around our area had been owned by a family named Carminati. He said many of the early settlers were Italians. When the parents died, the ranch had been divided up among eight kids - some since had been sold. (including his place, mine, and Jim Ed's. Milton's wife was his daughter and kept her 1,000 acres.

Truman thought the ranch north of me was still owned by one of the sons who now lived in Abilene. He said a feller from Nocona named - John leased it and ran a few old wild cows on it. (This later proved to be accurate).

Dale

I saved Dale last - plus he was the last one I met.

Dale bought the ranch which bordered the west boundary about two years after I had bought the T-Bone. It was in about the same run down condition as the T-

Bone and Dale was also a "weekend" rancher. He lived in Coppell, Texas and owned a dirt moving construction company. They were building a lot of houses in Coppell back then and he had plenty of work (and apparently plenty of cash also). His wife was a registered nurse.

Dale was a character - he was a tall lanky Oakie who dipped Copenhagen and drank beer - lots of beer.

The first year he came up every weekend and always brought two or three of his employees with him. However, he relied on my for tools - including my tractor and mower. Also, I fed them many a meal. I didn't mind - Dale was purty good company and he was always willing to help me when I needed him. Many weekends he would bring some of his heavy equipment up there (i.e. - backhoe, small bulldozer with blade, etc.).

One of his first projects was to construct a large barn. In the corner of the barn he built a real nice "apartment" that he stayed in. He had a well drilled and installed a septic tank - and installed a TV set with a tall antenna that would pick up the Dallas stations (i.e. - the cowboy games). He finally bought a brand new Allis Chalmers tractor and a mower and quit borrowing mine.

And lo and behold - one weekend when I drove into the T-Bone I looked over at Dales' place and saw a new house trailer all set up by the barn. Dale's truck and a car were parked by it.

After I got unloaded (I always had to take my food and water plus whatever supplies I would need for the weekend). Dale drove up and yelled.

I stepped outside and there stood Dale - grinning like a possum eating persimmons - with a can of beer in hand -

and spitting tobacco juice. Hop in the truck he said "I want to show you something."

I got in his pickup and we drove over to his new trailer. We went inside and he introduced me to his wife, Shirley, and his son, Ryan. Shirley was unpacking boxes and Ryan was watching T.V. Dale proudly announced they had moved to his ranch - permanently. I could tell the other two weren't as enthused as Dale seemed to be. (I was pleased cause now I had a permanent watch dog for my place.)

Comment and Update

Milton

Milton went back to work in about 1987 managing an auto parts store in Gainesville. I would see him leave about daylight and come home after dark. I felt sorry for him but Dale always said "He just loves money - he don't need to work - heck, he could stack his money up and climb up on top and see Dallas").

However, old Milton died in 2000 and before his body cooled his long lost son, Kenneth appeared and within weeks he had <u>two</u> new houses built on their ranch - one for the widow and one for himself and his new bride. He also bought a new pickup. It was apparent that old Milton had a few dollars stashed away.

As further proof, Kenneth has yet to get a job and has put on weight so it appears they are eating well. I rarely ever see any of them anymore. (Dorothy called me once after a violent storm to see if my electricity has gone out - it had at her place.)

<u>Truman</u>

Truman came over every few months for visits. He loved to talk about the good old days.

In about 1993-1994 he bought a herd of goats and two huge, white great Pyrenees dogs to tend them. The goats came through the fence and on to the T-Bone regularly but I didn't mind. They ate a lot of the saw briars in the woods that I was trying to get rid of. The big white dogs came over even more frequently.

However, after I got the house trailer and planted an orchard in the yard, I was forced to put a heavy duty woven wire fence around the yard to keep the goats out.

Dale was not as tolerant. He and Truman were always battling over those goats. Dale finally killed one of them and they quit even talking to one another.

I last saw Truman the weekend before he died (2002). He looked very bad and told me he had cancer and the doctor had told him he had about two months to live. (The doctor was a little over 7 weeks off).

Jim Ed

As previously stated, we never got to be friends and only met the one time. However, I can still hear his oil well pumps put-puttin and about once a year he gets a new pickup truck so I assume he's doing o.k.

John

My phone rang one night in late 1997. The party on the other end of the line said, "Mr. Thomas, you don't know me but my name is John. I lease the place north of you and run a few old cows on it. Another feller and I rounded up my cows today and have them loaded in two trailers - going to take them to the market in Bowie tomorrow. The reason I called is that we ended up with two more than I thought I had. In looking them over I found two baldy steers with a funny looking brand on them. I called Truman and he said they weren't his but he thought they might be yours - are you missing any steers?'

I told him that two baldy steers had disappeared from my place about 3 months ago - both had ear tags (#41 & #42) and had the T-Bone brand on their right hip. He said "That's them - I've got them loaded on my trailer so I'll bring them over to your place and take the rest to the Bowie livestock sale." I told him, if you don't mind, just take my two to the sale also and I'll pay you for your help." He said "Naw, I'd be happy to take them for you and you don't owe me a dime; where do they send you your check?" I said, "Just tell them T-Bone Ranch - I've sold quite a bit of cows there so they have all the information."

And sure enough, the next weekend when I picked up the mail, there was a check for $1,487.50 from Bowie Livestock Commission. I got John's mailing address out of the Nocona phone book and sent him a crisp $100 bill.

<u>Dale</u>

In addition to borrowing stuff from me all the time, Dale was always coming up with "deals". The ones I remember went something like this - (1) If I built a new fence between our properties, he would reimburse me for half the "cost." I did and presented him an itemized bill - including $200 for my time. He argued that was not cost

- to him, cost was out of pocket cost for the fence and posts - the labor was "free". He never paid me.

(2) He wanted to "run" his cattle on my place one spring so he could disc his up and plant grass - said he only wanted to leave them there till around July 4th and would give me a steer as payment. Sure enough, the cattle stayed on my place until about July 4th - of the following year. And he brought me a half of the steer which he had had butchered and processed in Muenster. His explanation was, he wanted to save me the "trouble" of butchering, etc.

(3) One day he told me "your pond sure needs cleaning out - I'm going to bring my back hoe up here next week and clean out my pond - don't you want me to clean yours while I'm at it? I said, "Yeah, that's ok with me." The next weekend there was a pile of "muck" stacked by

the pond and it contained numerous rotting fish - and there was an envelope taped to the door with an invoice from Dale for $1,000. I paid him that day.

(4) Dale was always trying to me to "go into business" with him. He had several ideas - build houses, open a tractor service business, buy a large ranch and raise registered limousine cattle, etc. (Dale thought I was rich - little did he know).

And of course, Dale was always fishing for free professional advice - particularly tax and legal. He was always giving me free ranching advice and it seemed to bother him that my pastures were always greener, thicker, and in much better shape than his and my cattle were always fatter and in better shape. (The reasons were simple - I had my soil tested and fertilized accordingly, I "aerated" pastures, and I fed the cattle "supplements" year round. - He did none of these things.)

In 1999 Dale came over and needed a friend. Shirley had left him and filed for divorce. I provided a listener for his sad story plus a fifth of Makers Mark which we drank. Dale concluded that he was going to sell out and go back to Oklahoma where he was raised.

And sell out he did - he sold his place to an American Airlines pilot named Victor and his wife Debbie. They were "weekenders" like me and I rarely ever saw them.

When Dale sold out he called me and wanted me to come over. I did and he showed me piles of junk which he had not hauled off to another place he owned near Nocona. He asked me if I wanted any of the stuff. I picked out some lumber, fence panels, posts, etc. and he told me he would let me have the stuff for $500. I said

"Heck fire Dale, I thought you were trying to give me that crap just so I would haul it off." He said, I need some money (for beer), how much cash would you pay. I said "I've only got about $100 cash on hand" and he said "sold". We loaded the stuff on my pickup and I paid him.

However, Dale finally got "even" with me. He had always complained and criticized my rickety front gate and told me I should put in a offset gate.

One weekend after he moved away, he must have brought his crew up with him and build me a very nice offset gate - and <u>did</u> <u>not</u>  leave an invoice. Also, he threw most of the old junk (lumber, pipe, railroad ties, old wheel barrow, ladder) across the fence into my pasture.

Then he vanished - don't know what happened to him.

CHAPTER 8

EARLY CONSTRUCTION PROJECTS

I had concentrated on the land itself long enough and with the tractor and mower had gotten the place looking reasonably presentable. (at least the weeds were mowed and Bermuda planted on front pastures). It was time now to start on the buildings. There was electricity run in to the old shack and I, had it turned on the first month. However, there was no water, telephone, sewage system, etc.

The first project I tackled was the old shack itself – it was a mess. I had already hauled off most of the trash so I could now concentrate on fixing it up so I could stay in it. Here is a list of the things I did:

1. Wired the house so I had electrical outlets in both rooms (it is a 2 room shack – L shape).

2. Patch up holes with flattened tin cans.

3. Cut out 4 windows and added windows and screens.

4. Added a front door screen.

5. Built a new porch.

6. Replaced the rusty stove pipe – one of the rooms had a wood burning metal fireplace in it.

7. Hired a workman to replace the roof.

8. Added a false ceiling made from Styrofoam sheets (a mistake).

9. Patched the carpet in one room.

10. Painted the floor in the other room and painted the walls in both.

11.Built a bed frame and bought a mattress and springs.

12.Bought a hotplate and toaster – maybe brought them from the Hideaway Lake House which I had sold – anyway, I brought pots, pans, dishes, etc, etc. from Hideaway).

I was to spend many interesting nights in the old shack until I finally got the more comfortable mobile home installed on the property.

As previously explained, the property did not have running water or a sewer system or phone (and cell phones were not available back then) so it was necessary to do something to solve problems created by these voids.

The first project I tackled was an "outhouse." Remembering the ones I had used many times in my youth it was an easy task to design it and no trouble to build it. The biggest problem was digging the hole in the rocky soil behind the shack. When it was finished, I painted it barn red of course.

On the trips to the ranch I had noticed a "surplus building materials" sign on a building in Sanger, Texas and one weekend I stopped to see what kind of stuff they had. I struck pay dirt! I purchased a shower stall and a commode seat and lid.

I rigged a plastic bottle with a short hose and mounted it on the plastic shower stall and had an outdoor shower (for warm weather only of course). I mounted the seat in the outhouse and that added to its comfort.

And finally, with the bucket attachment for the tractor I was able to haul rocks and dirt and fill in the storm cellar and get rid of the snake pit.

A few of the antidotes associated with the old shack follows:

1. The census taker

   One Saturday a stranger drove up to the old shack. I went out to meet her – she was an older woman who stated that she was working on the census (1990).

   She had a long form that she was filling out as I answered the questions.

   Finally, she came to a question - condition of house?" I didn't have an answer so she thought a minute and said "weathered?" I replied "Yep, weathered."

2. Shooting mice

   One of the never ending battles on the ranch has always been controlling rats and mice. I have gotten rid of hundreds of them with traps and poison.

Sometimes at night during the winter I would throw a couple of logs in the fireplace, put a slice of cheese on the floor, load my BB gun, and crawl into bed and wait in ambush for mice (and sometimes a rat) to sneak out of the darkness to try to eat the cheese. The fire provided plenty of light so when they approached the cheese I zapped them with a BB. Then I would have to get up and pitch them outside.

The next morning they would be gone – coyotes or bob cats had them for dinner.

3. Shahim the pyromaniac

Michael Shahim spent one weekend with me. He was fascinated with the fire. That night, every time it would burn down he would crawl out of his sleeping bag and throw another log on it. I finally went to sleep and was awakened during the night by a noise – Chop! Chop! I got up and turned on my flashlight, pulled on my pants, coat, and boots and went outside to see what was going on. It was Mike – he had dug up a big dead tree limb from the woods and was cutting more firewood. He had burned up my complete supply. He grinned and said "Bill - I just love a fire."

4. Thing to wake up to

Each morning as soon as I awoke, the first thing I would do was crawl out of my sleeping bag and paddle to the front door and step out to the porch to bleed my lizard. Then I would go back inside and put a pot of coffee on the hot plate to boil.

I remember the following things I saw as I first stepped out the front door:

- One crisp Fall morning the field in front of the house was full of deer - I counted 32 (including a large buck with 14 points)

- One Spring morning the field was full of wild turkeys – I didn't get an accurate count because they were moving about chasing grasshoppers – but I'd estimate 50 or more.

- Another morning I stood in fear and watched a large rattle snake slither from under the porch to the woods. I got the .410 and shot it.

I had seen many wild animals on the place but the quantity surprised me. I decided to post the place (no hunting) and create a miniature game preserve.

Deer

Turkeys

5. Things that go "bump" in the night.

One dark new moon night I was awakened by a strange noise. I sat up in bed, turned on my flashlight, and listened. Soon I heard the noise again – a distinct "bump". I shined the light in the direction of the noise but saw nothing. I sat there for minutes and it was silent – no more strange noise.

I finally switched off the flashlight and lay back down and soon dozed off – only to be awakened again by the noise. I fumbled around but couldn't locate my flashlight – however, I found my pistol which I kept under my pillow.

Soon the noise started again – bump, bump, bump – it was getting louder and coming directly at me – it seemed to be coming from the floor. It got almost to my bed and I let go with the 357 magnum – I fired all six shots at the noise – then I heard bump, bump, bump, bump – as the noise faded – obviously it was going away from me.

I located the flashlight, turned it on but saw nothing except fresh bullet holes in the floor. I put on my boots and went outside in time to see an armadillo emerge from under the house and go running toward the woods. (I figured out later that he didn't have much clearance under the house and the "bump" noise was made by this shell hitting the floor joists (beams).

Armadillo

Comment

The living conditions were very <u>crude</u> in the old shack – even harsh at times. The good things that came from the experience were –

* I developed a "feel" for what it must have been like for the early settlers and pioneers, and

* It made me appreciate all the modern conveniences we now have (air conditioners, running water, refrigerators, TV, indoor plumbing, etc.)

CHAPTER 9

SECOND ROUND OF CONSTRUCTION PROJECTS

One of the things I've always done is prepare "to do lists" and the T-Bone was no exception. My original list had about a hundred items on it and each weekend I would mark off a couple of them - then add others.

Anyway, the next go round of "construction" included the following items:

1. Tear down the hog pens and repair the metal building.

2. Tear down the pens behind the old shack and rebuild the small wooden building.

3. Tear down the pens by the pond and convert the buildings into a tractor shed and hay storage building.

4. Repair all the fences.

5. Fence off an area by the pond and start an orchard.

6. Build two corrals and install a head trap gate.

7. Paint everything - buildings white and everything else - red.

8. Put a sign by the entrance and fix up the entrance with something unique.

9. Build a barn.

10. Trim the woods so I could get through them with a tractor.

11. Get a computer.

Obviously, these projects were going to take a lot of time and hard work but not a lot of money.

So, the Spring of 1987 I got started. It became obvious that I needed help. I coaxed Michael, Kenny, and their cousin, Richard (Dickie) up a couple of weekends but they didn't last long. Also, Hamilton and Omar helped a little - but only a little. Free help wasn't the answer.

Me, Michael, Kenneth & Carolina

I placed a "Help Wanted" ad in the Montague "Shopper" and got about 20 responses. But, none of them panned out either. Most never came back after a day in the hot sun. A couple didn't even make it to lunch.

The only stubborn idiot that hung in there - was me. Slowly but surely I began to complete these projects and marking them other than killing a couple of snakes and getting stung a few times by wasps, the projects were coming along smooth. Well, now that I think about it, there was one exciting moment when I built the barn.

The place I selected to build the barn was at the edge of the woods, facing the front field. There was a huge oak tree that had a big limb hanging right where I wanted the barn - it had to come off!

I got my chair saw and a step ladder and drove down to the giant oak tree to perform the surgery. I set up the ladder, started the chain saw, climbed to the top of the ladder and started cutting the limb close to the trunk. Crrrr ack! The limb broke before I had sawed through and it swung around and knocked the ladder out from under me. As I was falling I had the presence of mind to shut the chain saw off and fling it aside before I hit the ground - no, hit the limb which had beat me to the ground.

I lay there and could not breathe. I thought I was going to die. Finally, when I was able to breathe there was a sharp pain in my rib cage and I couldn't move. I must have laid there at least 4 or 5 hours before I was finally able to drag myself to my pickup truck when was parked about 30 feet away.

I pulled myself up into the truck and drove to the emergency entrance at the Bowie hospital. a man helped me out of my truck and inside where a young doctor listened to what had happened, then had some x-rays made. He got the pictures back and said "Not too bad - a couple broken and a couple more cracked" so they (the doctor and nurse) took off my shirt and undershirt and wrapped me up then taped me and said "Get plenty of rest and I'm giving you a prescription for pain killers." I didn't have my wallet or any identification but told them if they send an invoice I'd send a check. They did and I did. This brought the construction projects to a screeching halt for a month or more - but I soon was healed and back at it.

I was able to finish these projects before Thanksgiving.

The two saddest projects that have occurred on the ranch have been burials. In 1995, my daughter Angelique's faithful dog - Taylor - died and we carried her to the T-Bone and buried her out behind the old shack. I put a wooden cross marker with her name on it on her grave. It rotted and I replaced it with a concrete marker.

Then in 2000, Ken and Gina, my son and daughter-in-law, had to put to sleep two of their dogs, Chows named Ms. Pepe and Babe, and they brought them to the T-Bone and we buried them next to Taylor. Ken had made a concrete marker for each.

Later, Michael buried a couple of his cats in the Cemetery. (Slim Jim and Princess) and of course - Chester.

Dog Graves.

I finally got a computer and Buzz came up one weekend and got it hooked up and gave me some lessons. I planned to use it to "write books." However, I really never learned how to use the darn thing. Finally, lightening struck it and ruined the main drive and it has gathered dust ever since.

I did do a lot of writing at the ranch - legal pad and pencil - on the kitchen table.

CHAPTER 10

THE FIRST HERD OF COWS

A goodly part of the credit for the further development and improvement of the T-Bone ranch goes to our client and true friend, Howard, of Palestine, Texas.

When we first got Howard as a client he was the 7th largest general contractor in the Dallas-Fort Worth metroplex and was worth about 15 million. However, it soon became apparent that he was in serious trouble and we joined him in his soon to be battle for survival. I could easily write a book about this battle (and may - later). However, the result was - he lost and ended up in bankruptcy. We managed to save his 1,000 acre ranch and some other property for him - but he lost his businesses and Highland Park home and he moved back to where he was born - Palestine, Texas.

Anyway, Howard was grateful for what we were able to salvage and knew we had written off a receivable from him in excess of $100,000.

He came up to the ranch one weekend and handed me a list of what he would do if it was his place.

1) Clear the woods

2) Build a house

3) Build a lake

4) Gravel the roads

5) Get some cows

6) Etc., etc.

7) Register a brand and join Southwest Cattleman Association.

I finally told him "Howard, I've already thought of all these things but there is a slight problem - I don't have the money to do them." He said "I'll help you."

I joined the Texas and Southwestern Cattleman's Association (Ft. Worth) and designed my brand and registered it in Montague. Now I was ready for cows.

About two weekends later he returned - pulling a cattle trailer with six young cows. We turned them loose and this was the start of the T-Bone herd. He said he would return the next weekend with a bull.

He did - not just a bull - but 2 young bulls. However, I knew his cattle sort of ran "wild" and figured these bulls were blood brothers to the young cows and was skeptical of what I might end up with if they bred - (maybe 3 legged calves, etc.).

So I turned again (as I had done for hired hands) and would do so many times later, to the good ole Montague Shopper for a solution. Two ads got my attention - one for a stock trailer and one for a young black bull.

L.D.

I bought the stock trailer from a German rancher near Muenster and drove over to the ranch near Stoneburg to look at the bull - which I also bought. However, when we tried to load him, he stepped right through the rotted floor of the trailer. The rancher had a trailer so we loaded him (the bull which I named LD, into his trailer and hauled him to the T-Bone ranch.

When we unloaded L.D., the girls (cows) seemed very pleased to meet him but the two boys (the Howard bulls) seemed very displeased. Matter of fact, they started to fight but it was no contest. L.D. outweighed them by at least 400 pounds.

I knew the herd mix wouldn't work and I turned again to the Shopper for help. I called in an ad - (Let's Trade - have 2 young Brangus Bulls - will swap for cows. I put my office number in the ad).

Then I went to Muenster and bought some good, treated 2x8's, and spent that weekend putting a new floor in the stock trailer.

The next week I received about a dozen calls in response to the ad - ranging from dairy cows to various cross breeds. The response that really got my attention was a rancher near Graham who had an old Brangus cow with a large calf and a Helford cow that was about 3 years old and currently "fresh." I talked to him (name of Hank) at length and was convinced he was serious about trading.

The next weekend Dale helped me catch and load the young bulls and I headed for Graham. I was to call Hank when I got there and I did - he drove up to the Fina station where I had stopped and I followed him to the pen where his two cows and calf were. I looked them over and he looked the bulls over before we started to horse trade.

I told him I didn't think the old black cow would live through the trip back to the T-Bone and wasn't interested in her. He allowed as how the bulls were awful thin. I could tell he really wanted them and he said he would trade - even! I said "No way - I might swap for $350 boot." He pawed and squirmed and finally said "Might give $100" I said "On second thought, I'm not sure I'd even swap for $500 boot." I asked "Is there a livestock auction in Graham?" He said "Yes, it's located on the north side of town." I said, well I guess I'll just leave the bulls there and let them sell them for me."

He said "Aw shucks, I'll give you $350 boot" and I said "Done". We unloaded the bulls and loaded the cows and calf and I headed back to the T-Bone.

The old black cow turned out to be wilder than a march hare but she got along ok with L.D. - she had another calf before I sold her. The Helford also hit it off with L.D. - immediately she had the first calf born on the T-Bone - Leroy!

LeRoy

Eventually, all of the cows had calves - all except one. She died giving birth.

Howard and William came up a couple of weekends later. We branded the cattle and put ear tags on them. They brought a welder and William patched up the mower and serviced the tractor. Howard asked, when are you going to start thinning out the woods? By then I had the fields mowed, trash picked up, and they (pastures) looked good - especially after I had spread a heavy dose of fertilizer on them. I told him we could start that project that weekend.

He declined, said he didn't bring a chain saw. I offered to go to town and buy another chain saw. He said "No, my back has been bothering me." He added "Next time I come up I'll bring William with his saw. He use to cut timber for a living." In a few minutes, he came up with another one of his "You should...." He said "There is probably someone around here who would cut the trees on the "half" for you." I asked him to explain. He said "Around Palestine, if you have standing timber you can find loggers (like William) who will cut the timber, haul off the logs to a sawmill and sell them and give you half the money, then clean up and burn the brush." I said, "There is a minor problem with your suggestion." He

said "What?"

I said "Just look at all these trees - they are all gnarly scrub oaks - no sawmill would buy them - they are too gnarly, knots, and crooked to get any boards out of them." Howard said "That's right - but you can sure get a lot of firewood."

So I placed an ad in the Montague Shopper and a Mexican named Joaquin Landoverde from Nocona answered  the add Thus began a mutually rewarding association that lasted the next five years. Joaquin had a family and lived in Nocona. He worked for a tree trimming company that cleared right of way for utilities, pipe line companies, etc. However, the work was sporadic and he welcomed this opportunity. One problem was - he had nothing to haul the firewood on so I shopped around and bought a 14' flat bed trailer for his use. He started coming to the T-Bone at every opportunity and before long, the appearance of the T-Bone began to change - it "opened" up.

He finished the tree clearing project in about six months then I hired him part-time (weekends) to help me. From that time forward. We got a lot accomplished each weekend - new fences, tore down hog pens, sheds, etc. -

filled in storm shelter. He was a god send and I paid him well. His brother, Santiago , also helped when we needed him.

Santiago suggested we build a couple of corrals to keep the water troughs in and to always feed the cows in the corral. (So we could capture them when necessary) after we brand them. I added a neck capture chute - for branding).

I learned from hard experience just how strong, stubborn, and stupid cattle (and horses) are. If I ever build another ranch I'll build things strong enough to hold an elephant.

CHAPTER 11

THE SURROUNDING COUNTRYSIDE AND TOWNS

I had passed through the area many times in the past - but mostly on IH 35 on U.S. 287. Both routes are through rather blah countryside. It wasn't until we had owned the ranch for several years and I started exploring the back roads did I really see and appreciate the beauty of the area. There are many rather tall hills and deep valleys.

The most interesting drives are state 377 between Saint Jo and Illinois Bend and a gravel road between Forestburg and Dye Mound - see photos.

The small towns and rural communities are (see map):

SAINT JO (APPX. POP 1,040)

Saint Jo, Texas

Where the Chisholm Trail cuts
the California Road

Saint Jo is the oldest town in Montague County - Founded in 1849. It was originally called Head of Elm. However, when it was surveyed and laid out in 1873, it is suggested the name was changed to <u>Saint Jo</u> because one of the surveyors named Joseph was a tetoler and his partner thought it took a saintly man to abstain. One of its earliest buildings is the Stonewall Saloon which still stands on the square.

This historical log cabin in Forestburg has been revamped.

Forestburg is one of the oldest towns in the county (1857). It was originally called Horn Hill. It suffered more Indian raids and brutal massacres than any other town in the county. The Butterfield stage line passed near Forestburg.

BOWIE (APPX. POP 5,400)

2001 Montague County Visitor's G

Second Monday Trade Days carries on a long history of trade and barter in Bowie. (Bowie photo)

Bowie is the largest town in Montague County. It owed its size and life to the railroad (1882) and later to U.S. 287. It's economy was first based on cattle, then cotton, then oil. Another interesting early industry was chickens (Johnson poultry ranch). In 1870 an Indian attack almost halted settlement.

Second Monday Trade Days began in the late 1800's and continues today. Downtown Bowie contains many antique shops and several banks.

MONTAGUE (APPX. POP 50)

Public Square   Montague, Texas   1904

The town of Montague is located near the Geographical Center of Montague County and is the County Seat. It was much larger in the early 1900's than it is today. It is driven by county Government today.

NOCONA (APPX. POP 3,200)

Nocona: Carved from the western prairie

Nocona, named after the famous Comanche chief, Peta Nakona, was settled by ranchers and the railroad greatly helped its settlement. Nocona later became famous for its leather goods - Nocona boot factory. (since closed).

CHAPTER 12

FAMOUS SIGNS

After I got things at the T-Bone about half way under control and had some free time on my hands I started driving around the back roads in the area. I "discovered" some very beautiful scenery and many unusual signs. Here are just a few examples:

Clay County:

A country road sign - Frog Holler Road

A town sign - Bugscuffle

Montague County:

Country Road - Seldom Seen Road

Poster in service station (in Montague) - Lost dog - 3 legged, black and white mutt, one eyed, ripped left ear - name ----- Lucky

Sign on fenced pasture containing huge buffalo - unless you can run the 100 in under 9 - stay the hell out of this pasture - the buffalo can.

I couldn't resist so I had this sign painted and placed by the front gate:

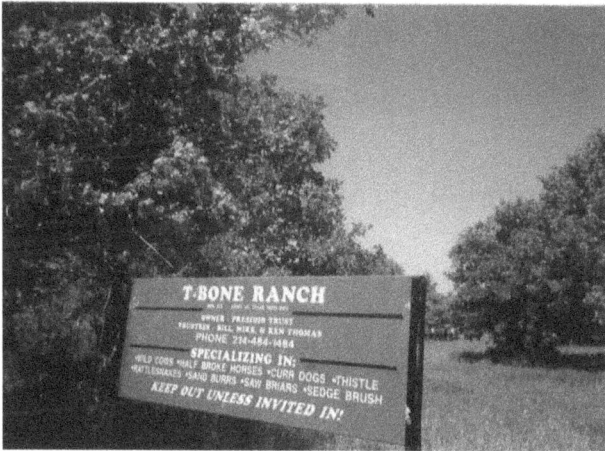

People used to stop, get out of their cars and go to the fence to read this sign and take pictures. I've seen as many as four vehicles stopped at one time by the sign.

Sign on Ranch Gate Near Newport - Fat Dog Ranch

Sign on run down looking

Farm near Slidell - Rainbow's End

Sign on farm gate near Bowie - Peckerhead Ostrich Farm

Even though Montague county and the surrounding area is one of the poorest (per capital income wise) areas of Texas, the folks are tough and have a good sense of humor.

Oh, almost forgot, there were two other signs on the T-Bone - on tree near entrance -

No trespassing - no hunting - no fishing - in other words - stay the heck out of here.

Tacked on wall facing front door (old shack) - over shelf containing jug of water and can of beans:

If you broke in here because you are tired,, cold, thirsty, or hungry - help yourself, build a fire, rest up -

then be on your way in peace - However, if you broke in to steal from me - think again! I'll track you down and break every bone in your body. Bill Thomas

CHAPTER 13

THE WILD MUSTANGS

I saw an ad in a magazine which had been placed by the Bureau of Land Management (BLM). they would give away wild mustangs which had been trapped further west - Montana or Wyoming I think. There was a catch - first, you had to supply proof that you had a good place to keep them and that you would treat them good and next you had to come pick them up - in Amarillo.

I responded by phone to the ad and the man who answered the phone said they didn't have any horses at that time but were expecting a new shipment in three weeks   and he would call me when they arrived. I said "Ok" and gave him my phone number.

The next weekend when I got to the ranch there was a message on my phone recorder. It was a man Jake in Wills Point, Texas who said he had two mustangs for sale. I called him and we started a horse trade over the phone.

First, I asked him how he got my phone number and knew I was interested in horses. He said he had called the Bureau of Land Management in Amarillo (where, it turned out, he had gotten the two fillies a couple of months earlier) and they gave him the information. I asked, "What kind of horse do you have to sell?" He said "Horses, I have two mustang fillies." He went on to describe how beautiful they were and I

interrupted him with "Are they broke?" He paused - then said "sort of."

He offered to let me have both of them for $500 - delivered to my pasture. I said "I think I'll just wait until the BLM gets another load of them and I could get one free - I concluded with - you got yours free too didn't you?" He said "Yes, but I've got feed, vet bills, and training costs invested in them and I'd like to recover some of my investment so I can buy the kids a 4 wheeler."

That gave me an idea - I said, "I might trade you a good 3  wheeler for them." He said "If it's in good shape I would consider a trade." He agreed to bring the fillies down the following Saturday.

I loaded the 3 wheeler into my pickup and hauled it to a Mexican (shade tree) mechanic, named Manuel, in Nocona to get it fixed.

A word about the 3 wheeler:

Howard had given me the 3 wheeler a few months before - not running and with 3 flats. Manuel had got it running and fixed the flats. I never did learn to ride it good - it was unstable and had a lot of torque. Just a couple of weeks before I had wrecked it and run off into a tangle of saw briars. It was skinned up, dented, had a flat, and wouldn't run - again. Thus, I was willing to spend a few dollars to get it fixed up and was delighted at the opportunity to get shed of it.

The following Friday I went through Nocona and picked up the 3 wheeler - it looked great. Manuel had touched up the scratches and polished it and put some armor all on the tires - it looked almost new - and ran like a singer sewing machine. I hauled it to the ranch and unloaded it.

The next morning around 10 a.m. I heard someone at the front gate  and looked up and saw a pickup pulling a horse trailer coming down the lane. I went out to meet them. The truck came to a stop by the old shack and a man and two teen agers got out. We exchanged "Howdies" and introduced ourselves. Jake was around 40 I'd guess and his son Jerry about 13 or 14 and his daughter Jennifer about 15. The horses were beautiful - but "wild".

Copper & Penny

They had on halters and were tied to the front of the

trailer. When Jake and I got close to them they tried to

rear up and one of them finally did - she broke the rope.

Jake called for Jennifer and she came over and finally got

her settled down.

I showed Jerry how to operate the 3 wheeler and he

rode off on it. Jake needed to go to the bathroom and

while he was gone - Jennifer told me the truth about the

horses.

Jennifer's story:

They had got the mustangs at the BLM three months ago and took them to their farm outside Wills Point. Jake had got them for riding horses for Jerry and Jennifer but they were wild. A man had tried to break them but finally gave up. She had fed them sugar and talked nice to them and she was the only one who could get near them. She had named them copper and penny. Some cowboys on horses had roped them and thrown them on the ground and finally gotten halters put on them but they had a hard time loading them in the trailer.

With this information I was ready to make a "horse trade."  When Jake returned it didn't take us long to complete the trade - 3 wheeler for 2 mustangs (easy trade - two motivated traders).

We unloaded the horses into a corral and loaded the 3 wheeler onto the pickup and they left.

I drove to Saint Jo and got a couple of sacks of horse feed and a box of sugar cubes. They had water and hay in the corral. When I returned they had quieted down but when I entered the corral with a bucket of feed they went crazy wild again. I dumped the feed in the feed trough and backed out of the corral. I tried to feed them sugar through the fence - but they wouldn't come near me. I decided to leave them penned over night.

The next morning I walked down the corral to check on them. they were settled down until I got near the corral and then they got crazy wild again. I swung the corral gate open and they came out of the corral like scalded apes and ran all around the parameter fence - looking for a way out of the pasture. They found none.

I put some more feed in the trough in the corral and decided the best treatment for them was no treatment - just let them stay wild if that was what they wanted. And that was what they wanted. I kept them on the ranch for almost a year and was never able to touch either of them.

Several so called "horse experts" had visited the ranch while they were on the place and all admitted they couldn't do anything with them.

Old Truman Weed put it best "once them sons of bitches grows up wild - they stay wild."

I finally put an ad in the <u>Shopper</u>

Will trade - two beautiful fillies for anything of value.

The best offer I received was a John Deere riding lawn mower so I took it.

Copper & Penny

CHAPTER 14

THE BIG BREAK - IMPROVED HABITAT

(FOR HUMANS)

Almost from the day I bought the ranch through the 1980's, the U.S. economy was terrible and the boys (Mike and Ken) and I were just getting by in our accounting practice in Dallas. There just wasn't much money left over to spend on the ranch. If you have been paying attention while reading this book - you will know that a lot of what I had accomplished up to this point had been done by "horse trading".

The first big break came in 1988 when Michael Shahim and I* were able to sell a company and collect a sizable commission. *We had a business brokerage company named Top Gun Business Sales. I spent most of my share on the following ranch improvements and adjoining acreage:

1) a 2 bedroom house trailer

2) a water well, pump, and water system

3) a septic tank and sewage system

4) buying many tools

5) another tractor trade and more implements

6) got a telephone, TV set, refrigerator, and freezer

First, I contracted with Hopson Brothers of Bowie to drill the water well and put in the water system and sewer system. There was an old water well in the middle of the south field but it was only 40 feet deep and didn't have much water - if you took a good shower it would probably dry it up. so we decided to drill a new well next to the old shack. They finally struck a good water supply at 270 feet and completed the well. They added a pump, built a well house, and ran water lines to both corrals and to the trailer site.

I had visited Howard Freeman in Palestine earlier. He was starting to get back on his feet with a new concrete company he started called Regional Concrete Company. he had a house trailer that he tried to sell me. I examined it and decided that it could be fixed up. The trailer had 2 bedrooms, large den, large kitchen and was 60 X 14. It had been built in Indiana and was well insulated and had central heat. I

decided it was worth the cost to have it moved to the ranch (over 300 miles) and the cost to fix it up. So I bought it and hired some movers, to move it.

When they showed up at the ranch with the huge trailer they could not get it through the front gate so we took a section of fence down and they brought it back to the tree line but could not maneuver it into the site I had selected. We ended up just pulling it as far into the woods parallel to the fence as they could get it. They leveled it and got it on blocks and anchored it down.

Fortunately, Hopson Bros. had not started the sewer system so all they had to do was reroute the water line. While they were doing the water and sewer I hired an electrician from Nocona to hook up the electricity and make the necessary electrical repairs to the trailer. I also had a telephone installed.

Furniture was no problem - we had a surplus of furniture in storage from the lake house (Hideaway Lake). I bought a new refrigerator and freezer. Also, we replaced the sink and gas stove and I bought a 200 gallon gas storage tank.

I spent all that summer fixing up the house trailer. The first thing I did was build a "skirt" around it at ground level. I built the framing out of treated 2/4's then covered with plywood. Next, I built a deck out of treated 2x6's almost completely around the trailer. Then, I had the roof coated and painted the outside white and the deck, skirt, and trim a barn red. I also replaced a couple of windows and the screens and added screen doors. And I added an observation tower on the south end of the trailer. I would climb up on it at night with a telescope and watch the stars.

Then I moved inside and went from one end to the other - replacing light fixtures, cleaning, and painting everything - walls, ceiling, trim, cabinets, etc. The floors were next - I put new carpet in the bedrooms and hall and new tile in the bath rooms. Then I put a linoleum tile floor in the kitchen.

By far the hardest project was putting a wood parquet floor in the den. That took several weekends and I swore I would never undertake such a task again. However, when I finished it really looked nice and was the taj mahul compared  to the old shack. Visitors must have thought so too because they started showing up on a more frequent basis. Some of them complained of the heat (which I had become acclimated to) so I bought and installed three window A/C units.

The roof later developed a leak(s) after a terrible hail storm so I had a metal roof installed over the trailer and it worked great.

My intention always was to build a ranch house - but I never was able to scrape together enough money to do so. However, the trailer was very comfortable and was all I needed . The house idea was for the family - who rarely showed up at the ranch anyway - except on July 4th.

One of the problems with the house trailer that a house would solve is running water in the dead of winter. Since the underneath of the trailer is not insulated or heated, the water pipes would freeze and burst in the dead of winter - Dec to March. Each year around Thanksgiving I shut the water system down and drained the pipes. I turn it back on each March. Therefore, I had to bring drinking water when I went up in the winter - and use the old outhouse which I moved down by the tractor shed. Winters weren't that much fun at the T-Bone.

Another aggravation has always been the well house. It is a little rinky dink thing built with concrete blocks. The only way to get into it was by lifting the roof (which must weigh 200#). I always had to use a jack and Ethiopian engineering to get to the switches to turn the pump off and on - and cussed the Hobson Bros. every time I did so.

I finally took a sledge hammer and knocked out a hole in the side of it that I could crawl through - framed it, and added an insulated door. It was much better but still a pain in the rear because of my bad hip.

When I took the first T.V. to the T-Bone the only station I could pickup was Lawton, Oklahoma and it was fuzzy - the rabbit ears antenna just wouldn't hack it. So, I bought an outside antenna and a pipe about 50 ft long and installed it by the fence. It didn't work all that great either - Lawton came in clear but it wasn't a network station and I could also get Wichita Falls and DFW - sometimes. Both fuzzy plus I had to manhandle the antenna to turn it.

Lightening finally solved the problem. It struck the antenna and burned out the TV set. I did without for a couple of years and finally got dish TV - it worked great.

Speaking of T.V. - Hamilton still reminds me of the super bowl weekend he and I spent in the old shack. I had a small T.V. with "rabbit ears" and assured him we could pick up the super bowl. But when I turned the set on all we got as the buzz sound and "snow" on the screen. I tried to build a T.V. antenna out of coat hangers and aluminum foil and was finally able to get an occasional flicker of a picture but no video. He still talks about that hardship.

CHAPTER 15

THE WEATHER AND SEASONS

Among the many differences you notice out in the country - as opposed to the city - is the weather.

In the country, the seasons become more pronounced. In the winter you notice all the bare trees and dead grass - everything is dead and brown. And the cold is colder - principally because you are outside more. The cows usually drop calves late January and February. The coyotes songs are mournful in the winter. The deer don't venture out much. But when it snows, the ranch is gorgeous. It usually snows once (or more) each winter. The earliest snow was late in October and the latest snow was in mid March. However, because I shut the water system down in the "freezing" months (Dec. to March), it is not that <u>comfortable</u> staying at the trailer so most of the time I just go up to check things out and return to Dallas.

But the snow added another dimension - it was very pretty.

House trailer

Hay

Corral

Ken & BoBo

Barn looking West

Backyard

Pond

There is nothing like spring - the trees start to leaf out, the grass starts to leaf out, the grass starts growing and turning green, and the wild flowers bloom profusely. The cows start perking up and the new born calves become playful. Spring even has its own special smell - a smell of <u>life</u>. The migrating creatures start returning. First the robins - they are all over the place hopping around on the ground, scratching for a worm or grub. now and then a northbound flock of geese passes overhead - sometimes they stop for a rest and land on the lake. Then the hummingbirds return and I hang out their feeder - they congregate around it in droves. In mid April the wild turkeys start their mating and you see and hear them all over the places. I get out my turkey call and literally call them up to the yard. Sometimes the toms get into a fight and the feathers fly. The girl turkeys merely stand by and watch and wait for the winner to be determined - who they accept as their next boyfriend.

But with the good there also is the bad. The springtime storms can be fierce! The ranch is along the southern boundary of "tornado alley) and hardly a spring has passed that a tornado or two hasn't touched down near the ranch. Each spring I expect one to visit the T-Bone. One thing I've noted is that the storms are cyclical. Some years are much worse than others. (The locals blame this on el neeno).

Fact is - the T-Bone sits in the middle of "Tornado Alley."

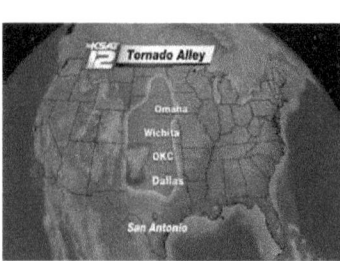

Tornado Alley

Bad News

Some tornado and stormy experiences

One spring day I was discing the front field I noticed
that the wind had died down and it was very calm.
However, the sky was taking on a greenish color and
dark clouds were building in the west. Soon I heard
thunder and saw lightning flashes and the wind picked up
as the clouds rapidly approached. I speeded up the
tractor - trying to finish the field before the storm hit. I
heard a strange noise overhead and looked up. A tornado
was foaming - literally directly over me - perhaps 2000 ft
up. I stopped the tractor and watched the tornado build
and move off in a north easterly direction. It started to
rain and hail so I rushed to the barn and took shelter.
(The tornado touched down near Muenster and did
considerable damage).

During another storm, I think it was the same year - perhaps 1997 or 1998 - I was in the trailer and listening to the weather radio. They said a tornado was on the ground south of Montague. I went to the window on the south end of the trailer and looked out - and saw the damn thing. It was a dark funnel moving west to east and was across the road from the ranch - I could see trees and other debris fling around the terrible funnel. After it and the storm passed, I drove over to look at the damage. There was a long cleared strip through the wood about 100 yards wide - as far as you could see. It looked like a cleared "right of way" - except there were uprooted trees and broken limbs everywhere. That one only damaged the woods.

The storms without tornado were bad enough. They were the worse when they struck at night. Many times I have been awakened by the thunder, lightning, hail, and high winds. The old trailer would be taking a pounding and would be rocking - like a ship at sea. Many a tree around there has the scars of storms past (struck by lightning).

The ranch is about the highest elevation in north Texas (appx. 3000 ft A.S.L above sea level) and is just asking for lightning strikes. Lightning has struck at the trailer twice when I was in it - once it hit the transformer on the utility pole by the trailer (knocking out the electricity of course - that's why I have an old fashioned kerosene lantern handy).

The other strike was when it hit the TV antenna next to the trailer and burned up the TV set. That time I was sitting at the kitchen table and it scared hell out of me. One thing I learned - lightning has an odor. You can actually smell the ozone like odor for several minutes after it hits.

But the worse damage is done by the wind. There is no telling how many times I've had to gather up sections of corrugated metal roofing and re-nail it back on roofs. I've finally learned to put 2x4 bracing on the edges and use screws and washers instead of roofing nails.

And of course, I've picked up truck load after truck load of limbs and stacked and burned them later. Mother nature keeps the trees pruned. (Not really)

After the stormy season passes it starts warming up - naw, it starts heating up. It gets hotter hell during the summer. By then I turn native - and run around like an Indian in a breech cloth (actually - a ragged old bathing suit). I get browner than a biscuit and stay brown till winter.

The hot weather doesn't bother me. I acclimate to it quite well and much, much prefer it to cold weather. Because of the elevation, greenery, and blowing wind - it always seems at least 10° cooler at the T-Bone than in the concrete jungle called Dallas. For years, I didn't have air conditioning at the T-Bone - and didn't really miss it. But visitors complained so much that I finally installed 3 window units in the trailer. However, unless I have guests, I usually just raised the windows and opened the doors and don't even turn the air conditioners on.

In the hot summer I drank a lot of water and dill pickle juice and eat salt. That's another problem I have with visitors - the well water. It has lots of minerals in it (hard water) and most visitors don't like it. They end up driving to town and buying bottled water (which had become quite the fad).

One trick I taught myself is "I fill plastic bottles with water and freeze them. Then when I'm driving the tractor or working I'll take three or four of my bottled ice with me - all day long I have ice water to drink.

There are two things bad associated with the hot summer weather - drought and sand burs. Drought, like tornados, seems to be cyclical. Most years there is enough summer rain to keep the grass growing to support the cattle. But every few years it just don't rain. It gets so dry and dead that fires become a very real threat. The county adopts a "No Burn" policy - with good reasons. I've seen a few grass fires that burned up hundreds of acres and when the grass is gone - you either start feeding hay or get rid of your cows. Neither solution is good - I've tried both. If you have to buy hay I've seen it get to $100 a roll (normally $30-40 roll). Twice I've been forced to sell off all the animals (cows and horses) after they had eaten every blade of grass plus all the leaves they could reach on the trees. Hungry cattle make a mournful sound - and bring a very low price on the market (everyone is selling). It's bad and costly.

There ain't nothing more aggravating than a dad blamed sand burr. They are little round monsters with needle sharp spines - look sort of like a miniature ship "mine." They attached to your breeches leg and hurt - and are deadly on socks if you happen to be wearing low cut shoes. It's very near impossible to get rid of these pests. I've tried all kinds of weed killer - nothing works. I've even tried to dig them up and burn them - but they come right back. About the only thing I've found to do is keep them mowed down and try to keep them under control. (If someone has a better solution - I'm all ears.)

Ah, but just when you are about ready to give up on mother nature and the hot dry weather - fall arrives. It rains and cools off. The grass greens up again and day time temperature drops down into the 80's and at night it drops to the 60's. An occasional cold front drifts down from Canada bringing more rain and cooler temperatures. The snakes start crawling out onto the gravel roads to warm up - and many are executed by pickups. All the wild animals become friskier and more active. The coyote serenades take on a joyous sound. The leaves start changing color and the scenery is something to behold . In late fall the geese start passing overhead - heading south. The hummingbirds disappear - as do the monarch butterflies. It is quite a sight to behold to see a "flock" of monarchs heading south. I've only seen them once but I'll never forget it.

The fall is the time of year to start preparing for the cold weather which is just around the corner. I get all the pastures mowed down close - first to try to get rid of the weed seed - and second, to get rid of fuel for grass fires. I also do maintenance on all the equipment - lubricate, change oil, change filters, add anti freeze, sharpen blades, etc. and store it out of the weather till it is needed in the spring.

Fall is the most enjoyable time of the year on the T-Bone.

CHAPTER 16

TREES, PLANTS AND VEGETATION

The predominant trees on the T-Bone are oak - a variety that I call black oak. They covered the place except for the front field, when we first got the ranch. We have gotten rid of most of them. Oak trees produce acid and it is difficult to get anything else to grow near them - the exception being the Bour de arc, a tree tough as iron, with long thorns, and a large (grapefruit size) seed called "horse apple." Deer and squirrels eat it. There are also many cedar trees.

It seemed like that most of the native plants were there to harm you. The saw briars (some call them green briars) grew on every fence and every tree. They could really rip you and your clothes up good if you got tangled in them. And you invariable got tangled in the darn things.

Thistle has "needles" that can darn near cripple you when you get them in your socks.

But the most aggregating plant of all if the sand bur. If one of them even got in bed with you - I guarantee you couldn't sleep a wink. Or if you got out of bed at night and stepped on one you had tracked in - I guarantee it would wake you up. I truly <u>hate</u> sand burs.

I have tried since day one to get pecan and fruit trees growing on the place. The first orchard I planted was down by the tractor shed. I planted peach, plum, cherry, apple, and pear trees. At first, rabbits chewed the bark but I put chicken wire around the trunks and stopped that. I hauled water (from the pond) to irrigate them. But, one by one, the trees died.

After we got the house trailer (and water system), I planted the next orchard in the yard. I put a metal wall around the base of each tree so I could fill it with water (hose) and it could slowly soak in. However, most of these trees also died and it has become a spring ritual - replanting fruit trees. One peach tree made it to maturity and produced about 3 bushes of peaches one year - the squirrels and birds got most of them.

I have planted perhaps 2 dozen pecan trees - all over the place. Only two have survived. I planted some willow trees by the lake and they are doing well. And, Michael started some mimosa trees in a bucket and I transplanted them on the ranch - one planted in the back yard survived.

For the first few years, I religiously planted a garden behind the old shack. I planted a variety of vegetables -

tomatoes, green beans, corn, carrots, radishes, black eyed peas, etc. All summer long I would haul water from the pond to irrigate. Then, when it came time to harvest - the deer, squirrels, birds, and rabbits harvested it. I was fortunate if I got a tomato and a mess of beans from my garden. I finally gave up. Now I plant about 6 tomato plants in buckets and keep them close to the back door of the trailer - and guard them with a BB gun.

As to the pastures, I have planted Bermuda, rye, fescue, vetch, and red clover, the most success has been with Bermuda. However, the clover took over on the east hillside about three years after I planted it. I let it grow and seed out and it came up the next year - and the next - and the next. I finally cut it last year before it seeded and got rid of it. I now have Bermuda all over the ranch - although it is spotty on the east side.

The year we built the lake, I took a bag of wild bird seed and scattered it in the "burn piles" (where we had burned the tree limbs). The next year we had sunflowers, milo, gourds, cantaloupe, and who knows what growing in those piles.

Once I ordered some seed for a plant from New Zealand that was supposed to attract big bucks. It produced a plant about a foot tall that had a broad leaf and tasted like cabbage. The deer loved it. It didn't reproduce.

My experience with shrubs (around the trailer) has been similar to the fruit tree experience. The only thing is the old reliable - wax leaf ligustrum.

Among the wild plants my favorites are:

* Blackberry vines
* Wild flowers - Indian paint brush, bluebonnets, and numerous
    others I have not identified.
* Buffalo grass

The pests (which I discussed in Chapter three) are:

* Sand bur (I hate)
* Saw briars
* Thistle
* Johnson grass

My latest experiment is a plant (name unknown) which some clients from India gave me that is supposed to grow anywhere. I've planted some along the barren shore line of the lake and in dirt heaps that Howard left when he "cleaned out?" the ponds. We'll see.

Soon after the house trailer was added, I started an orchard. However, during the 110 plus degree days in July and August I always lose several fruit trees. I replant them in the winter. Today, the orchard consists of the following:

6 - Peach trees

4 - Plum trees

4 - Pear trees

4 - Apple trees

6 - Fig trees

8 - Pecan trees

4 - Grapevines

CHAPTER 17

ANIMAL BEHAVIOR - WILD ANIMALS

I've spent the majority of my weekends at the T-Bone alone. (in various Chapters I've described weekend guests). Well, I really wasn't alone - there were also the animals (domestic and wild). I've spent many an hour observing them - and enjoyed it immensely. I always keep binoculars handy. Here are some of my observations.

<u>General</u>

It is my observation that animals spend most of their waking hours searching for food or sex - so humans come by these traits naturally I suppose.

DEER

Even though the deer are not hunted on the T-Bone Ranch they remain quite wary and stay hidden in the woods mostly during the daylight hours. They start venturing out and come to the feeders just before dark and feed in the open pastures at night. When they are feeding at night the congregate into a herd. It is not unusual to see from 12 to 15 sets of eyes in a spotlight at night. They usually stay out until after daylight.

Often the doe's have twin (2) fawns. When they are very small the fawns either stay very close to their mothers or she will hide them (usually in tall grass) while she grazes and visits with the girls. If there are any boys (bucks) with the herd, they are normally young boys. The old boys stay by themselves. As the young get older they become very playful and venture off from their mothers.

If anything disturbs them, the older doe's snort (blow through their noses) and stomp their feet. If they decide there is danger about, they throw up their tails and run for cover. As long as you don't make any sudden movement, they normally don't run when they detect your presence (i.e. - smell you). I think they must recognize my odor for they come right up in the yard while I'm sitting on the porch.

And the older doe's aren't afraid of Chester* either. I've watched him run at them, barking his puppy head off, and the old doe's start running - at him! He tucks his tail and runs back to the picnic table and climbs on top of it - his haven.

There is an old 14 point buck that lives on the ranch joining the T-Bone on the north boundary. I would see him occasionally - either right at dark or in the truck headlights. But, come first frost (around Halloween) it is not unusual to see him trotting across the ranch - nose to the ground trailing a doe who is about ready for some sex.

*See Chapter 18

SQUIRRELS

The woods are full of squirrels. There is a squirrel family that lives near the trailer. They visit the bird feeder every day and eat the seed I put out for the birds. I've also built a squirrel feeder and keep it full of corn and pecans - but they persist in stealing the bird seeds - even though I chase them off - and Chester barks at them.

About the second year that we owned the ranch, my granddaughter Carolina found a baby squirrel in our back yard. She brought him in the house and we fixed him a bed in a shoe box and fed him with one of her doll bottles. He survived and prospered. She named him

Rusty. I built a cage for him and when he got bigger we fed him vegetables and nuts. One day he got out of the cage and nearly destroyed the house - he climbed the drapes - knocked over a lamp - etc. My wife said "Rusty has got to go!" So - I took him to the T-Bone. I built a house for him and nailed it on the big tree by the kitchen window - and built a little feed platform where I placed nuts and corn. It was late fall when I took him up to the ranch and for months after that I could go out on the porch with a handful of pecans and he would come to me and take the nuts out of my hands.

Winter came and Rusty quit coming - he had abandoned his house. But the next spring he showed up - with a mate. Rusty had apparently gotten married that winter and joined the wild squirrels. Even today there is one grown squirrel that comes to the bird feeder by the trailer and doesn't run when I step out on the porch. He won't come to me but he doesn't flee either. I think it's Rusty.

WILD TURKEYS

I see a few turkeys near the pond and tractor shed year round. In fact, one turkey mom had her nest in some tall weeds by the tractor shed for 3 or 4 years and raised her chick's there. They scamper off into the deep woods when they see me. Sometimes I see some crossing the dam at the big lake.

One evening late, Howard, William and I were sitting on the dock, feeding the fish, and an old turkey hen came walking across the dam. She was followed by four half grown chicks and they were followed by a smaller hen. (apparently the nurse maid). The procession got almost across the dam before they saw us. They did an about face and retreated back across the dam and gathered in a group. Then they came marching back across the dam in their original order and when they were nearly across they broke into a run and disappeared into the woods. (It appeared they had a meeting and decided, by golly - they were going to cross that dam - human beans or no).

On another occasion in the early years, I woke up one morning in the old shack and looked out into the big front pasture and saw about 50 turkeys. They were feeding on grasshoppers. Here again it appeared they planned their strategy. They were in groups of 6 to 10 and would walk abreast until a grasshopper would fly up and a couple would chase it until they caught it - then they would re-join the line.

But come April - turkeys are everywhere. They come into the yard and eat the corn from the deer feeder. You hear them "gobbling" from every direction - it's mating season. I have a turkey call and I get it out and call the old gobblens up every year. I've watched them come from different directions - sometimes meeting and getting into a big fight - right in the yard.

When I was putting in the parquet floor in the trailer (Chapter 14), I was on my hands and knees and looked around at the open door. Something popped up and then down. It looked like a cobra at first. I waited and it popped up again - a turkey gobbler. He was just curious about what was going on inside the trailer (which had recently invaded his space).

Turkeys, like the deer, come right in the yard while I'm sitting on the porch. As long as I sit still they are not disturbed by my presence. However, any sudden movement and they run for cover.

RABBITS AND QUAIL

Both rabbits and quail seem to be cyclical. Some years they are in abundance and in other years there aren't any. Can't explain it - but that's the way it is. when they are in abundance I like to sit on the porch and answer the Bob Whites as they call "Bob, Bob, White" from the pastures. Sometimes they come right up into the yard - looking for the female who was responding to their call. And often a covey would come into the yard - the baby birds were not much larger than a chocolate covered cherry with legs.

When the rabbits were in abundance, I could never grow a garden. They ate everything I planted. They also ruined many fruit trees by eating the bark.

COONS

Raccoons have always been a challenge. They get into everything. they destroyed many a sack of cow feed before I learned to store it in steel 55 gallon drums. Heck, they even got in the steel drums - until I learned to put a heavy rock on the lids so they couldn't take them off. Then they crapped on the lids to let me know what they thought.

There was a large hollow tree down by the creek that was a den tree. One year I saw a baby coon sticking its head out of a hole - about 15 ft up the tree. I used to go down there and hide about 50 yards away and watch 3 baby coons play. Finally, old mama coon would come out and chase them back in the house (den).

There was one big old boar (male) coon that gave me trouble with the hummingbird feeder that hung by the kitchen window. It took me a while to figure out what was happening and a while longer to put a stop to it.

I would fill up the feeder with hummingbird "juice" (boiled water, sugar and Kool-aid) and hang it out. It held about half a quart. The next morning it would be empty. (Normally it would last a week). I would refill it - next morning - empty. I thought, have I been invaded by a flock of giant hummingbirds? What is going on?

The next weekend when I filled it up I sprinkled <u>flour</u> under feeder. Sure enough, the next morning the feeder was empty but the mystery was solved - there were white coon tracks all over the deck.

So, I filled the feeder again and set a steel trap under it. The trap was wired to the deck rail. During the night I was awakened by a commotion on the front deck. I got a light and my trusty .22 rifle to go see what was going on. When I shined the light there was one of the largest coons I had ever seen - with a front foot caught in the steel trap. I put a bullet between his eyes and the next morning I threw him out in the pasture for buzzard bait.

Last coon story - I have a recliner chair in the den that I kick back in to watch T.V. at night. Almost invariably I fall asleep in that comfortable chair - wake up around 2 or 3 a.m. - get up, bleed my lizard, and go back to the bedroom and go to bed. (I wake up after a short nap and get up around 4:30 or 5 a.m. to make a pot of coffee and start the new day).

One night in the hot summer, I had opened a package of Fritos and put some in a paper plate which I took, along with a small can of bean dip and a coca cola, to the recliner and munched on while I watched Friday night fights. I had left the remainder of the Fritos in the opened package on the kitchen table. All the doors and windows were open (no air conditioning at that time) as usual I fell asleep in the recliner but something woke me up around midnight. I sat up and listened to the noise coming from the kitchen. It sounded like paper crinkling and tearing and a crunching sound. The kitchen was dark and there was only the light from the T.V. in the den. I hobbled to the kitchen and shined the light toward the racket.

There sat a big coon – munching on my Fritos. I hobbled toward him with my flashlight and cane. The light blinded him a I was able to get close enough to whack him with my walking stick before he jumped to the floor and took off down the hall – me cussing and chasing him. He disappeared in my bedroom.

I turned on all the lights and popped a small door open before I continued on my coon hunt. I finally located him under my bed and poked him with the cane. He took off back up the hall and escaped through the open door. I threw the chips out and cleared up the mess he had made – then went to bed.

Just remembered <u>another</u> coon experience – this one is very similar to the Frito story except it involves two coons.

I admit that it was my fault creating some of the "situations" I'm writing about – so what!

I have bad habit of throwing "table scraps" out the back door. As a consequence, I always attracted neighbors dogs, stray dogs and cats, coons, possums, skunks, armadillos, etc. to the trailer.

One night I was awakened by these terrible screams. I sat us in bed and listened it sounded just like a woman screaming – and it seemed to be coming from the kitchen. Truthfully, I was scared. I turned on the light, grabbed a flashlight and my .22 rifle and crept up the hall toward the kitchen. The screams were getting louder. By the time I got to the kitchen I determined the screams were coming from outside the kitchen door (screen door – again summer time).

When I got to the back door and shined the light outside there was one big ball of gray and black fur bouncing around. It was two big coons fighting – probably over the table scraps. I started to shoot them but decided to yell instead. I yelled and they quit – then I shot into the ground and they took off for the woods. I figured I scared them <u>almost</u> as bad as they scared me.

SKUNKS

When I was a boy I had a close encounter with a skunk and got "sprayed" so I had a great respect for their "weapon" and avoided them whenever possible.

You rarely saw them during the day but it was likewise a rare event if you drove anywhere at night without seeing one. And you saw dozens of dead ones along the roads and highways in Montague county that had been run over by cars. Montague county must be the skunk capital of Texas – if not the world.

To me, skunks are a pure nuisance. I'm sure the good Lord put them here for a purpose – but I don't think his purpose was to aggravate me. I shoot the little devils every chance I get. That (and snakes) is the reason I keep a .22/410 in the pickup.

I've probably trapped at least a dozen of them. They dig holes and get under the old shack, the metal lumber storage building, and the house trailer.

You have to be careful when you trap them. I set the trap where they have dug to get under the building. The trap must be secured (tied to a stout peg) so they can't pull it under the building when they are caught. When you catch one you have to sneak up to a safe position where you can see them and shoot them In the head. If you don't kill them instantly – they stink up the place.

If I never see (or smell) another skunk I'll be happy.

COYOTES

I like to hear the coyotes sing their mournful songs at night. It gives the place a true western feel. Visitors are always fascinated when they hear them. Many ranchers hate them and even hire professional trappers to get rid of them. They have never bothered me and, except for one I shot when I first got the ranch, I don't bother them.

I know for a fact that they catch and eat rats and mice. One afternoon I was mowing a pasture that had grown up high with weeds and I saw several rats scamper through the weeds ahead of the mower. I caught a glimpse of movement out of the corner of my eye and looked toward it. At first I thought it was a stray German Sheppard dog but after looking more carefully I knew it was a coyote. He followed the tractor until I finished mowing at dark and I saw him catch and eat seven (7) rats that scampered out into the mowed areas. (see also hawks).

On other occasions I have watched coyotes through my binoculars as they hunted rats in the pastures when we first got the T-Bone it was overgrown with weeds and infested with field rats. By keeping it mowed and with the help of coyotes – the rats are about all gone.

My most unusual experience with the coyotes occurred one cold frosty night. There was a full moon. I had gone to bed early (not unusual) and was sound asleep but something woke me up. I listened to the most mournful sounds you could imagine – and they were very, very close. It was spooky! I got out of bed and hobbled over to the window and looked out.

The coyotes were having a convention in the <u>yard</u>! There must have been 25 or 30 of them – all shapes and sizes.

I just went back to bed and covered my head with a pillow and went back to sleep.

<u>WILD HOGS</u>

I had put a deer feeder in the woods – along the creek bank. At that time we were running mostly brangus cattle and were probably "over" stocked. The cows kept knocking the feeder down and eating the corn. To remedy this, I built a woven wire fence around the feeder to keep the cows out. (the deer could easily jump the fence to get to the feeder).

For several weekends I noticed that something was rooting under the fence to get to the corn. At first I thought it was an armadillo but one night as I was driving to the ranch and started down the hill toward the creek the road came alive with little black critters – running helter skelter in the blindness headlights. They were wild hogs!

I had heard ranchers from Jack County complaining about them but had never heard anyone mention seeing them in Montague County. So, I spent most of one weekend watching that feeder. (I had a folding chair and binoculars and was on the hill – about 100 yards away from the feeder).

Sure enough, at nearly dark. I saw movement near the feeder and when I looked through the binoculars I counted 8 wild hogs at the feeder. The puzzle was solved for certain.

I didn't want to shoot them and – the next time I saw Truman I told him about the wild hogs. Truman said, "There's an ole boy I use to work with who traps them wild hogs and sells them." I asked "Do you think he would be interested in trapping the bunch of my place?" Truman said, "I'll call him and find out."

Later that day I got a call from the wild hogs trapper. (Can't remember his name – he had a small place on the Oklahoma side of the Red River - across from Illinois Bend). He was interested so I gave him directions to the T-Bone.

He showed up the next morning – rolling his "hog trap on wheels" behind his pickup. We hauled it down by the feeder and got it set up. He baited it with "soured" corn.

He left and said he would come back the next morning to check it. I decided to stay an extra day at the ranch in order to be there when he came by.

He showed up the next morning around 9 o'clock and I went with him to check his trap. Success – he had caught one. He hitched the trap to his truck and left with the porker. But for whatever the reason – he never came back – neither did the wild hogs for a month at latest.

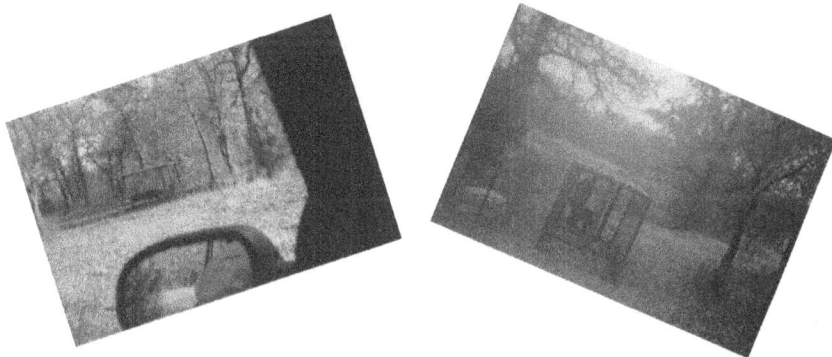

I later mentioned wild hogs to the gunsmith who I used and he said that he also trapped hogs. I invited him to trap on the T-Bone and he caught ten (10) of the pesky pigs. However, there remains dozens of the devils.

179

EMUS

There was a craze going around in the mid "90's about Emus and ostriches, (part of the health craze – low fat diets, etc.) I got all sorts of advertising literature in the mail about ostriches and emus. You could get rip roaring rich – raising those birds. And you could get started in the business by buying just one pair of these birds for just $20,000. But heck, as soon as the hen laid one egg – you could sell it for $5,000. I even went to a ranch near Pilot Point that was selling those birds. But I never bought any. But many folks did.

The fad lasted for a couple of years before the bottom fell out – the suckers holding the bag (birds) couldn't even give them away –it cost more to feed them than they were worth. I'm sure some folks just opened their gates and shoved them out – they became wild again.

One night I was coming up Hwy 455 and topped a hill about 5 miles north of Forestburg. My headlights came down on a big emu standing in the middle of the road. I braked and swerved to miss the bird and darn near wrecked.

For a year or two it was not unusual to see those big birds out in pastures and along the roadside. But over time they began to disappeared.

One spring morning I was sitting at the kitchen table, drinking coffee and smoking a cigarette (sound familiar?) when I heard a racket. I went outside to investigate and the fence was shaking. About 50 yards north of the trailer, the bushes across the fence (on Truman's place) were shaking. I couldn't figure out what was going on so I went back inside and got the .410 shotgun and went to investigate.

What I found when I got close was an emus that had gotten tangled up in the thick saw brains along the fence. I went to the tool shed and got my trim saw on a pole and went back and was able to cut enough of the vines to free the old bird. He trotted off into the woods.

Later that morning I heard a "K-boom!" from Dale's place. I knew then what had happened to all the "wild" emus.

BOB CATS

Bob cats are nocturnal creatures and are very wary little critters.

In Chapter 2 I described shooting one the very first night I spent on the T-Bone. But I never shot another one – although I saw a few.

Just about everyone I saw was at night – in the headlights of the truck.

One afternoon late when Omar was visiting, we went down by the pond and sat on the tailgate of the pickup and I blew on my weems wild game call. I was able to call one up. It approached through the woods from the direction of the creek. Omar shot at it – but missed.

I feel the same about Bobcats as I do coyotes – they don't bother me so I don't bother them. It is much more enjoyable to see them occasionally than to shoot at them.

POSSUMS

Another wild creature that I see once in awhile – usually at night.

Every now and then one will try to take up residence under the trailer . I pitch a few mothballs under the trailer and they vacate the premises.

Possums are blah – not worth writing about.

ARMADILLOS

Armadillos are another critter that fail into the nuisance category. They wreck havoc in the yard – digging for grubs. In one night one armadillo can literally dig holes all over the yard. But they are small holes and a good rain will fill them up and the grass grows back.

Life coyotes, some ranchers kill them every chance they get. I don't. I tolerate them cause they too add some "western flavor" to the place.

Visitors are fascinated with them and its amusing to watch Chester chase them and listen to the "clacking" as he tries to <u>bite</u> them through their tough armor.

RAPTORS – HAWKS AND OWLS

In the early years, there were a lot of hawks and owls on the T-Bone. Like the coyotes, they were feasting on the abundance of field rats.

There is a large oak tree in the middle of the front pasture. In the early years it was not unusual to see one or two hawks sitting in the tree every time I mowed that pasture. Whenever a rat tried to escape the mower by running out into the freshly mown area – one of the hawks would swap down and catch him in his talons and take him back to the tree for a snack.

One day I chased a long black and yellow ringed snake out of the weeds and watched as a hawk swept down on him. I was curious to see if the hawk would try to take him back to the tree also. He didn't . The snake coiled up – ready to fight – and the hawk spread it is wings and bounced around and jumped on the snake, sunk his talons in it – then ripped its head off with his sharp beak. He then proceeded to eat the snake there on the ground.

One morning I was sitting at the kitchen table, drinking coffee and smoking a cigarette, and watching a young squirrel hopping across the lawn – coming to raid the bird feeder. He never made it – a hawk swept down and caught him in its talons and flew away with him.

I've been outside, watching the squirrels and birds on the feeder when a hawk would fly over and give his call

– "Kressee!" All the little critters disappeared and took cover.

Owls are nocturnal but you could find them during the day of you listened for the crows. Anything you hear a bunch of crows "caw" "cawing" and raising heck if you slip up on them they will have something "treed" – and 9 times out of 10 it will be an owl.

One day as I stepped out the door I heard such a crow convention down by the pond so I slipped down that way to see what was going on. Sitting on a dead limb in a big tree was the largest owl I had ever seen. It had something in its talons. I stepped out into the open and walked toward the tree. The crows flew away followed by the owl. Whatever it had in its talons fell to the ground. I walked up and examined it – it was a partially eaten cat. (Milton was right – Chapter 7).

SONGBIRDS, ETC.

I have a bird feeder in the yard and a Hummingbird feeder hanging from a tree limb and they attract all kinds of birds. The regulars include:

*Blue Jays   *Cardinals   *Chickadees

*Doves   *Finches   *Hummingbirds

*Marking birds   *Martins   *Robins

*Sparrows   *Red headed wood peckers

Plus, a little green colored bird that I've never identified in a bird book.

In addition, I have two Martin bird houses and they are full of purple Martins during the warm months.

The sparrows are pests. They try to take over the martin boxes.

And of course, there are always many hummingbirds around their feeder. There are two kinds - grey one with a black head and a colorful one with red head. They sometimes have aerial combat over who is going to get the nectar in the feeder.

DUCKS, ETC.

After the lake filled, migrating ducks began landing on it and I began feeding them. I scattered shelled corn along the bank in shallow water. Most of the time the ducks were mallards.

I also saw a few wood ducks a couple years.

The Canadian Geese and Sandhill Cranes flew over the ranch - but never landed.

And I saw many Cranes - year around. They were trying to catch small fish and minnows - and often succeeded.

One day I watched a Kingfisher for a couple of hours. He dove time after time at the feeding fish but I never saw him catch one.

FISH, FROGS & TURTLES

After the lake was completed I stocked it with bass, bream, channel catfish, and minnows. I added a fish feeder and began feeding them. Many times I sat on the dock and watched the fish eat them.

Mother nature supplies the frogs and turtles. I gigged a few frogs and fixed fried legs - delicious eating.

The turtles were a nuisance and I shot them with my 22 rifle to keep them under control. (Also shot a couple of water moccasin snakes.)

SNAKES

When I first began clearing the property it was infested with snakes - particularly copperheads. I killed many of them with my trusty 22/410 over/under and many more with the mower. The fire got a few but I believe the thing that really chased them off were the feral cats that homesteaded the old shack.

I only saw two rattlesnakes and killed both - one at the old shack and one when the lake was being built.

I have seen several king snakes but protect them - they are good snakes.

Finally, have only seen (and killed) one water moccasin at the lake.

Conclusion

Several visitors have commented "That T-Bone ranch is really a game preserve – and I suppose it is.

CHAPTER 18

OMAR – THE MIGHTY HUNTER

I met Omar Lennon through Hamilton Rial in the late 1980's. We hit it off from the start and I invited him to visit the T-Bone. He showed up a few weekends later in an old Dodge sedan. The weekend he came up, I was building a fence and he pitched right in and helped me. The only problem was – he wanted to help too much. His motor was revved up and he was trying to do the work of a 25 year old field hand – and he was 3 times that age – he was 75. Over time I was able to teach Omar two things; first, old folks should just <u>piddle</u> along and not get in a big hurry and second, there was more than one way to skin a cat. Piddle was a new word added to his vocabulary and he used it often.

Omar became a "regular" visitor to the T-Bone and he was always welcome. I enjoyed his company and he always pitched in to help me with whatever project I was working on. I always had to explain whatever I was doing in great detail. For a long time I thought he just wanted to learn – later, I figured out that wasn't the reason at all. Omar was a creative genius** and he was always trying to invent a "new" tool to help with the work. It's rather ironic that the two "new" tools he dreamed up to help in fence building – had already been "invented." One was a fence post puller and the other was a bob wire unroller. When I showed them to Omar he was amazed that an accountant like me could build such contraptions. Here is what I had built:

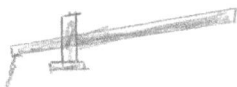
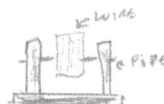

Fence post <u>puller</u>.   Bob wire <u>unroller</u>.

I don't profess to be the inventor of either tool. I saw a
TV program about the Amish farmers in Pennsylvania
and they were using a gadget to pull fence posts which
was similar to the one I built. It is no more than a simple
lever with a chain attached to the short end to wrap and
tie to the fence post. You merely push down on the long
end and it lifts a metal fence post right out of the ground.
The bob wire unroller was copied from a gadget I had
seen some Mexican fence builders using years before out
in west Texas. It was no more than a frame which sat in
a pickup bed that allowed you to slide a metal pipe
through a roll of bob wire and place it in the frame so you
could pull the end of the wire and unroll it from the

tightly wound roll. (the secret was to drive the truck very slow so as not to get "backlash" on the roll.

Omar and I used to sit on the porch late in the evening and talk about the "good ole days" and watch the deer feed at the corn packed deer feeders. Omar grew up in Kansas – the son of Russian immigrants. His father was an itinerant "lightning rod" salesman. When he got out of school he went to work at the Boeing factory in Wichita, Kansas – building B-47's. He later knocked around the country – earning his living as a salesman. He had married and raised a daughter who now lived in California. His first wife died and a couple of years before I met him he had re-married. He and his wife, Shirley, lived in Carrollton. (the things we had in common were Kansas, hunting, fishing and B47's). He had invented a packaging machine for bread wrapping and worked for years for the company which manufactured the machines (Hamilton had been one of his salesman).

Some of his other inventions included a closet rack that maximized closet space for storing clothes, a wire tying gadget to tie steel rods used in concrete support, peanut butter in a toothpaste tube, and a zippered hunting suit.

Omar had a goat beard and it, along with his hair was white (gray). He had a twinkle in his eye and an impish smile. There was a remarkable resemblance to Col. Sanders of Kentucky Fried Chicken fame.

We talked a lot about hunting. Omar used to tell me all kinds of wild tales about his going on an African Safari with the folks from the Oklahoma manufacturing Company. He had shot a lion, elephant, Oryx, and several other species. Several times he had "hinted" about deer hunting on the T-Bone (even though I had "posted" signs nailed to nearly every tree).

I finally decided to let him hunt so when the next hunting season rolled around I told him "Omar, why don't you bring your gun on your next visit and thin out some of these deer," he lit up like a kid with a new bicycle and said "that's great – sure you don't mind" I said "Sure I'm sure."

On the next trip he had the old Dodge loaded down with hunting gear – you would have thought he was going on another Safari. He had several guns, boots, knives, hunting costumes, and a bolt of camouflage cloth. I helped him select and build a couple of "deer stands" – using the camouflage cloth. Every weekend during hunting season he spent the early morning and late evening hours in those deer stands. However, as the weather got colder he moved to a more comfortable stand – the old "outhouse" down by the tractor shed. It commanded a good view of the young orchard and a feeder.

I set up about five deer feeders – mostly to attract deer for Omar. However, I have continuously fed the deer the year round ever since.

While Omar was out freezing his butt off in his deer stand, I stayed in the cozy trailer and read or watched T.V. and drank coffee. When he came back to the trailer he would be nearly frozen. After he got out of his camouflaged hunting costume, drank a cup of coffee, and thawed out he always had an exciting story about the big one that got away – always an excuse though – scope fogged up, gun jammed, deer spooked and ran into the woods, etc, etc.

One weekend Omar had some sort of car trouble and got there late. He had not eaten and I had not cooked anything so we decided to go to town (Bowie) to eat. There was a problem – everything was closed. I suggested we drive down to Decatur – a much larger town. He said "ok." We stopped at a barbeque joint that I had tried before and went in. It was one where you went in and these was a walkway around the wall you followed to the food counter where you pleased your order.

Omar asked if I had eaten there before and I told him I had. He asked next "what do you recommend?" (I remembered a funny sign that hung on the wall just this side of the food counter and we were only a couple steps away.) I stepped up to the sign and pointed to it and said "I recommend this highly."

Fresh road kill – armadillo – barbq to perfection. Omar said "No thanks – I had that yesterday." He was very quick witted.

I remember another occasion when he and Hamilton Rial spent the night in the old trailer with me. The trailer had a metal roof on it. It was very windy that night and a tree limb hung right over the guest bedroom. We had already gone to bed and I heard him get up and saw a light from his flashlight shinning down the hall. I yelled and asked him if anything was wrong. He said "there is something on the roof making a terrible noise." I got up, put on my britches and boots and got a flashlight to go investigate. The noise was being made by the tree limb rubbing the two roof when a gust of wind moved it. The limb was about the size of my wrist. And I did not feel like getting a ladder and saw to get rid of it.

Omar and Hamilton had come out to observe and Omar said "If you have a saw I'll climb up there and saw that rascal off." It was rather cold and the limb was about 20 feet up so I said "I've got a better idea." Omar said "What?" I asked, do you have plenty of bullets for your deer rifle?" He said "Whole new box."

I said, bring your 30-30 rifle and a handful of bullets. He did and handed them to me. I said "Hold the light on that limb about a foot from the main trunk." I loaded his rifle and proceeded to shoot the limb – in a vertical line. After about 6 or 7 shots "crack" and it came crashing down. Omar looked at Hamilton and said "He's done it again."

Omar hunted for four or five seasons and never fired a shot. I'm positive he really did pass up many opportunities but I suspect he had gotten like me – he was no longer mad at the deer and just didn't want to kill another one.

Omar died in 2001 – I still miss him.

CHAPTER 19

BOY, HAVE I GOT ANOTHER GOOD

"DEAL" FOR YOU

One of my all time favorite cartoons was one by Ace Reed, the famous cowboy cartoonist. I'm no artist but maybe you'll get the gist of it from my crude replica.

Slim, I am glad to see you - boy have I got another good deal for you.

The character on the left is me and the one on the right is Charlie. In Chapter 5 – I described my first "tractor trade" with Charlie. There were several more after that one.

The old 9N Ford tractor that I had swapped Charlie out of didn't make it through the 90 day "warranty" period. It just quit running. I called Charlie and he and one of his shade tree mechanics came out and tinkered with it all one afternoon and couldn't get it to running. Charlie finally gave up and said "Bill, we're going to have to take it back to the shop where we have the tools and equipment to get it fixed. I really don't know what's wrong with it but it seems to not be getting gasoline." I said "Fine." (He knew the gate combination and could come in anytime – he said they would pick it up Monday and deliver it back later in the week).

The next weekend when I got to the T-Bone - no

tractor. I went over to Dale's and used his phone to call

Charlie – no Charlie. I talked to his son who said "Dad's

out of town – buying trip – back next Monday." I asked

about my tractor "He wasn't for sure but thought they

were "waiting on a part."

What could I do? Nothing – just let the weeds grow

taller.

Same scene – following weekend. The only difference

was, I got to talk to Charlie. He hemmed and hawed and

finally said "I got the old tractor running but it ain't got

no power – it needed overhauling real bad. I asked

"How much?" More hemming and hawing. He said I

can't say for sure until we take it apart but it could run 5

or 6 " hunnert ." I started cussing and he interrupted "I

know how you feel so don't make a decision right now – I'll call you next week sometime."

Sure enough, the following Wednesday I get a call in my office from Charlie. He started with "Boy, have I got another good deal for you." That alone should have been ample warning to hang up on him but I didn't and he continued "You really need a bigger tractor for that place of yours. I located an ole boy down in Sunset that has a good looking McCormick 50 horsepower that I can trade the 9N for – with a little boot of course. He's out of work and has the tractor tore down now and has been overhauled from one end to the other. However, he ran out of money and still needs some rings, inserts, bearings, etc. I can get all those parts and have it put back together and at your place by Saturday. What do you say?"

I said "I say, what did you say? What's the deal?" He

said "Like I said, I can trade your 9N plus --- say $600

and maybe another $100 for parts – for a real fine

McCormick 50 h.p. – your

9N is only 30 h.p. (new) –

now about 3 h.p. you

reimburse me the $700

and get a practically new tractor".

I said "Charlie, I've never heard of a McCormick

tractor. He quickly responded "It's the same as an

International Harvester – except it was made in England.

(Another bad sign that I missed). I said, "Wait till I come

up next week end and we'll go look at it – then I'll

decide." He said "That will be too late – the ole boy has

a back up- cash offer for his tractor and he gave me till

noon today to trade – else he will sell it to the other feller" (another missed clue).

Silence.........

Charlie then came back with the clincher. "Heck, you can pay me what you can now and give me a note for the difference."

Without thinking I said "Deal".

The next weekend when I drove into the gate I looked toward the old shack and the tractor was parked next to it. I changed to my work clothes and came out to examine my new toy. It sure wasn't much for looks. The paint was faded and worn down to bare metal on the hood – and rusted. The fenders were nearly rusted off. The tires were badly worn. I ran the battery down trying to get it started – then I called Charlie.

Charlie tried to put the blame on me "he said, you should have called before you started messing with it so I could come out and show you how to operate it." Now you've run the battery down and we can't start it – that motor has been overhauled and it's tight and hard to turn over." Do you have a battery charger?" I said I did so he said "Leave it charging all night and I'll run by sometime tomorrow and help you get it started."

I said Charlie, I need to start mowing weeds - now! How the heck do you start this darn thing – I'll jump start it with my truck battery." Charlie cooly responded "Just settle down – get a pencil and paper and write down what I tell you." I pretended to be getting pencil and paper and delayed before responding "ok" Ready".

Charlie said "First, check the oil, water and gas – we didn't put but about of gallon of gas in it – next, open the gas shut off value (under the gas tank, next to the settling bowl, pull out the choke, black knob left of key on dash, pull the throttle open about 3clicks, then step on the starter, floor by clutch – she should fire up after 3 or 4cranks. If it don't – call me."

I did as Charlie instructed and he knew what he was talking about – it was low on liquids – 2 quarts of oil, about 3 gallons of water, and the gas tank was dry as a bone. When I added the liquids I found out that all 3 were "leaking" – the radiators was the worse so I added some "stop leak." (later I replaced the washer on the oil drain plug and the gas line connector to the settling bowl. Everything stopped leaking except the radiator and I just kept adding water as long as I had the tractor).

I hooked up the jumper cables and cranked the old McCormick and she started – ran purty good too. I had hooked up the bush hog (mower) before I tried to start it. So a mowing I went. The old tractor ran good and it was noticeable more powerful than the previous old clunkers I had mowed with. All I has to do was steer – no more down shifting in the patches of thick Bermuda.

The biggest problem with this tractor as it turned out, was tires. The rear tires were worn down practically to the cord and the front ones weren't much better. The rear wheels were an odd ball size and Charlie could not locate any new tires in that size anywhere in north Texas. He said we would probably have to import a set from England. When he told me the cost I said "No thanks." He gave me the name and number of a man out of Bowie who would come to the ranch and fix flats.

I got by that summer with "fix a flat" (tire repair goop in an aerosol can.) However, on a cold, rainy day in

December I struck the pickup in the mud down near the pond. I chained the old McCormick to the truck to pull it out and when I started the pull the tractor started spinning its wheels. Then pop – a flat. The tire had uncovered a sharp metal object which punched a hole in it.

It was on a Sunday morning and I had to get the truck out if I was to return to Dallas so I reluctantly called the repairman – not knowing what to expect. To my amazement he said he would "be right out." In less than an hour this battered old truck pulled up and this grizzled, bear like man got out and introduced himself (Jim Ed). He had on old greasy canvas coveralls, boots, and a tobacco cap and the cold rain didn't seem to bother him. Before you could say "scat" he had jacked up the tractor and removed the wheel. He grunted and banged around on it and finally removed one side of the outer tire wall from the rim. He put a large boot over the hole but before he remounted the tire he recommended an inner tube be added since he feared the tube might leak. He had a used tube in his truck – not the right size but he said it would work so he put it in, put the tire back on the rim, started his air compressor and soon filled it with air. We smoked a cigarette and waited a few minutes to see if it was going to leak It held so he bolted the wheel rack on and helped me get the truck "un struck".

Maybe "helped me" is not a proper explanations. He unchained the tractor an told me to get it "out of the way" (which I did) and he moved his old truck into position and hooked a cable from his winch to the pickup and winched it out.

I asked him "How much?" (I figured he would say at least $50). He looked at his feet and shifted around and muttered "Aw about $25." I answered "What?" He took my reaction to be negative and he became more vocal and defensive and said in a louder voice as he gave me a challenging look "twenty five dollars – twenty for labor and five for the tube." I pulled out my wallet and handed him a $50. He looked at it and said "I ain't got no change." I said "You don't need any – it's all yours." He thanked me profusely and got if his old truck and in departing said "Any time you need me – just call and I'll be right out."

(I had learned over the years that it was extremely difficult to get anyone from the surrounding towns to come out to the ranch to do work. Further, for the most part, the towns were almost closed on the weekends – and really closed after 12 on Saturday. That forced you to either plan ahead and get whatever you needed in

Dallas before going up or missing a day of work and go up on Friday morning. Also, any time I succeeded in getting a repairman to come to the ranch - I tipped them well so they would return if I needed them.)

About a year after I traded for the old McCormick I stopped off at Charlie's place of business (Saint Jo Tractor) to deliver his tax return. He had six huge John Deere tractors on his lot – they were all the same models – just alike – diesels, cabs, etc. I commented on them to Charlie and he smelled another trade with old Bill. We walked out and inspected them and Charlie started one up. It sounded good (I love to hear and smell a diesel running anyway). Charlie said he had bought these six from a dealer in Mississippi. Said they were trade-in's by a big cotton farmer who got new tractors every three years. Charlie allowed as how he had bought thee tractors "right" he could let me have my pick for the McCormick and $5,000 cash. After a lot of jockeying around I finally gave $4,000 – on a payout deal.

They brought the John Deere out and picked up the McCormick I didn't realize how large that John Deere was until I climbed up in it and started it up. I literally could not get it through the woods to get to the tractor shed to hook up the mower. I spent the rest of the day with a chain saw – cutting down trees and tree limbs so I could get it through the woods. I also had to make a run to Bowie to buy a couple of 5 gallon cans and get diesel fuel. By the time I got the mower attached and the John Deere fueled up I was able to make two passes around the big front field before it got too dark to see. I parked the tractor and went to the house.

The next morning I was up at the crack of daylight and fired up the big John Deere started mowing. What they say "nothing runs like a Deere" is true. That big ole tractor could pull that mower around field in high gear – it was <u>very</u> powerful! I had the pasture mowed before noon (it took all day before with the McCormick and a day and a half with the Ford 9N).

Charlie must have made a bad deal with our last trade for he tried several times to trade me out of it or buy it back outright. (Later, I found out that he sold the other 5 John Deere's in less than a week and had several orders (cash offers) for John Deere's. They were very popular – especially at his price.

Charlie, with my help, was able to take on a line of new tractors called Zetor. I think they were made in Czechoslovakia. He tried every way he could to get me to swap the big John Deere for a new Zetor. I wouldn't trade. He finally asked "Just what in heck would you trade for?" I told him if he even came across a small Ford diesel in real good shape – I "might" trade.

Several months passed and I got another call in my office from Charlie  who said "I got your tractor" He went ahead to describe the Ford 3000 diesel with less than 100 hours on it. He claimed that he bought it from widow woman up in Oklahoma and picked it up from her barn where it was on blocks. He said her husband had died a few weeks after he bought the tractor and it had been in her barn ever since. He gave me her name and phone number. I told him I would stop by his business Friday afternoon and look at it.

I called the lady in Oklahoma and she confirmed Charlie's story. I asked her when her husband died. She said "1985". That meant the Ford was about 15 years old. When I drove into Charlie's on Friday the Ford was parked out front. They had cleaned it up and it looked like a brand new tractor. I checked it over and the only things I could find were dry rotted tires, dead battery, and rats had chewed on some of the wiring. I decided to trade if Charlie would be reasonable.

I said "What is your offer?" He said "the John Deere plus $2,000 cash." (Charlie seemed a little bit "uptight"). I said "You're out of your mind – I wouldn't trade even." He replied "No even trade – what's your offer?" I said

"Put new tires and a new battery on the Ford and I'll swap even." He said "Can't do that" so I climbed into my truck and started backing out. He yelled "Stop! If I put on the new tires and battery would you give $1,000. "I said "Heck no" and started backing again. He yelled once more "$500?" I stopped, opened my briefcase and wrote a check and handed it to him. He promised to deliver the tractor "in the morning".

When I pulled in the gate at the ranch the first thing I noticed was "No John Deere" – it was gone. My first reaction was – darn I've traded with Charlie and now can't deliver on my end of the trade. I went inside and called Charlie immediately and he chuckled and explained "I sold your John Deere Tuesday morning and stole it from you – I was going to tell you but you drove off so quick I didn't get the chance." I just hung up.

Then I called a mechanic in Nocona and he agreed to come out next morning and check the Ford 3000 out front to rear.

Miguel (the mechanic) got there early so he joined me for coffee and cigarette while we waited on Charlie. I explained the history of the tractor. He said because it had been sitting so long we should drain all the fluids and flush it out an change the filters. While we were discussions this, Charlie came through the front gate with my "new" old tractor. He unloaded it by the old shack and said he had to get back so I said "Go". Miguel had been walking around the tractor – giving it the once over. As Charlie left, Miguel said "This is a new tractor – better than new - they don't make them this good anymore. He predicted. You will never have to buy another tractor – this one will last the rest of your life (so far – he was right).

I got some buckets and Miguel started draining the fluids (oil, hydraulic, and anti freeze). He asked me to get paper and pencil and make a list of what we would need so I did. The list included (1) Delo oil (2) anti freeze (3) hydraulic fluid (4) oil filter (5) fuel filter (6) glop lug (7) electrical wire and (8) diesel fuel. I already had a grease gun. I decided to drive to Decatur to the Ford tractor dealer (McMaster) to get the stuff. Before I left I noted the real wheels seemed too close together. Miguel said they could be flipped and he would do that while I was gone. So I heated for Decatur.

When I returned, Miguel was finished and waiting for the stuff. He had "flushed" the systems. He immediately began replacing the glow plug and the damaged wiring.

Everything completed, I climbed aboard and tried to start it – nothing. It wouldn't even turn over. Miguel checked it out and said it wouldn't start in gear or with the kill switch pulled. I took it out of gear and pushed in the red knob (kill switch) and tried to start. It started immediately and ran like a Swiss watch – nice.

And it's been running sweetly ever since. I love that little Ford 300 diesel tractor – it is a prized possession - and by far the most dependable piece of equipment on the ranch.

Comment

The only problem I've ever had with this tractor is the hydraulic; Got sluggish and erratic. Charlie's mechanics tried to fix it but only made it worse. Finally, William (Howard's dozer operator), took it about one weekend and replaced some gaskets and filters – and its back "Just like new." Oh, almost forgot – did have to replace the battery recently and of course, have had a couple of flats. Otherwise – it's been perfect.

CHAPTER 20

HORSES AND COWS AND COWS AN HORSES

Horses and cows are rather stupid creatures. They are clumsy and destructive. If I ever build another ranch from scratch (highly unlikely) I'll build it as if I were going to run elephants. Everything would be "Heck for stout" - especially fences. And anything on the property that was not for grazing would be fenced off. I've had them destroy a barbecue pit, an orchard, and the yard plus they crap on everything. I've always said "I'm thankful that cows don't roost in trees."

Horses (including Wild Mustangs)

   *We have owned six horses - two each time.

   *First were the mustangs - Copper and Penny. I told you about them in Chapter 10.

   *Roman and Cleopatra (Cleo):

   *Mamasita and Pedro

Next were Roman and Cleopatra. Roman was, by far, the finest of the horses we owned. He was a large, majestic, and beautiful animal (see photo below). I saw an ad in the Dallas Morning News - "Horse for sale - owner desperate." I called and the owner was a nurse up in Sulphur Springs. She told me the horse was a Missouri Fox Trotter and he was large (17 hands), broke, gelded, and gentle. She had raised him from a colt and trained him. She was getting married and moving to Los

Angeles and had to get rid of him - now. She was asking $2,500.

I told her I was interested in buying him - but could not afford $2,500. She wanted to know where I would keep him and who would take care of him." I told her I would take care of him and I described the T-Bone. She volunteered to bring him to the ranch for inspections - me to inspect Roman and she to inspect the T-Bone.

When she drove up in her Cadillac pulling a fancy horse trailer I figured the deal couldn't be made - she obviously didn't need the money. But after we met and she unloaded him, I knew I wanted that horse. She also brought her tack so she saddled him and I swung into the saddle and rode him around the ranch for a few minutes. Then I rode back to her, dismounted, and started horse trading. I ended by paying $1,500 for the horse and the tack. She claimed the only reason she let me have him so cheap was because she felt he would have a good home on the T-Bone and that I would take good care of him - which I did. She cried as she drove off. I felt sorry for her.

Roman was a good horse and despite his size - he was gentle as a pussy cat. And boy was he a smooth ride - just like a comfortable rocking chair.

Roman

However, after a few weeks Roman started acting sad - at least that was my diagnosis I had Dr. Porter come out and check him over - he gave him a couple of shots but said "Nothing is wrong with him." I told him about his apparent sadness and about his former owner that had raised him from a colt. Dr. Porter agreed with my theory and said - you should consider getting him a playmate - another horse. Sounded like good advice to me.

The next second Monday I went to "trade days" in Bowie (pulling my trailer) and headed to the animal section of the trade grounds. There were 4 different ranchers there with pens of horses for sale. I looked them all over purty good and settled on a bay quarter horse mare that looked about Roman's age (4). He wanted $1,000 and I offered $500. We kept horse trading until we closed the deal at $600. He helped me load her and I took her to the Cross Timbers Vet Clinic for Dr. Porter to check her out He did and gave her a couple of shots. Then we headed to the T-Bone.

When I went through the gate Roman was clear across the pasture. However, he must have smelled her and he neighed and ran toward us. By the time I fastened the gate he was beside the trailer - smelling, whining, and making a fool of himself. Cleopatra (that's the name I came up with) didn't seem all that excited. So I unlocked the trailer gate and let her loose. She took off across the pasture with Roman close behind. With Roman, I think it was love at first sight. But it took a little longer with Cleo. I think she knew he was a stud dud.

Cleo was ranch broke and not near as gentle as Roman. When you did succeed in getting a saddle on her (which was very difficult to do by myself), she would crow hop and buck a time or two before settling down. I learned that the best thing to do was swing into the saddle, spur her good, let out a squall and and whack her across the rear and let her run full out for a couple of minutes before pulling her up. That took the edge off and she would settle down after that.

Cleo

I enjoyed these two horses more than any we owned. My hip wasn't too bad then and I was able to ride and several visitors who came up also rode them. But they were somewhat expensive to keep - they ate like - well------horses.

When the drought came and the cattle and horses ate everything edible - I elected to "sell out." I ran an ad in the Dallas Morning News and got numerous responses. A couple drove up from Dallas in their Mercedes followed by their trainer in his pickup truck pulling a horse trailer. He said he owned an electronics company (which was flying high at the time) and he and his wife had just started riding and loved it. They wanted "show horses." They asked for "papers" on the animals. I had no papers but I made up a big story about their blood lines, etc. and winked at the trainer (who appeared to be a good ole boy).

The man finally asked "How much?" I instantly replied "$5,000." He started to try to Jew me down and I said "each." That started him so he took a time out and huddled with his wife and the trainer. They broke up and he asked "Can we ride them?" I said, if you mean "may we ride them?" I said sure. I got some feed and put it in the feed trough in the corral and penned them. Then I went to the old shack and got the tack - the trainer came along to help. I asked him if they were experienced riders and he chuckled and said "Heck no - they're rich Yankee's that haven't been on a horse a half dozen times in their life." I told him Roman was no problem but Cleo might be. I explained how I rode her. He said "Let me handle it." (I figured then I had a done deal).

We saddled the horses and led them out of the corral. He jumped on Cleo and tore out across the pasture with her. Then he rode back to me, dismounted, gave me her reins, and mounted Roman and did the same. The buyers sat in their air conditioned Mercedes and watched.

When he rode back up he waved for them to come over and he helped the woman up on Cleo and I helped the man up on Roman. they rode around the ranch for at least an hour while the trainer and I sat in the shade, drank beer, smoked, and shot the breeze. He had a little place outside Denton and boarded and trained horses. He would take care of these two if they bought them - and he thought they would.

When they rode up and dismounted the man said "We like theses horses but I don't think I will pay $10,000 for them because they don't have papers." I said "What would you pay?" He said "Not a cent over $7,500." I said "Sold for $7,500." He wrote me a check and they loaded the horses.

Before they drove off, the trainer (out of earshot of the Yankee's" said "You stuck it to them good - and that's good" - and they drove off. I didn't feel that good about it - matter of fact I was sad and felt like crying (as the nurse had done who sold Roman to me).

Mamasita and Pedro:

The last two horses on the T-Bone were an old quarter horse mare and her colt.

After Charlie sold me the Ford 3000 tractor and finally concluded he was not going to trade me one of them new Zetors - he switched his tact.

Charlie caught me eating breakfast at the Dairy Queen (Saint Jo) one morning - got himself a cup of coffee and joined me. We shot the breeze for a while and he finally asked "What kind of horses have you got now?" (Heck, he knew I didn't have any - in a small town everybody knows your business - especially your inventory). I said "Naw Charlie, I don't own any horses now and don't need any."

All he heard was the first part of the sentence so he continued "Boy have I got a good deal for you - I took in this quarter horse mare, Cutter Bill bloodline, used to race and won a lot of money, and she's bred to one of them Dash for Cash horses. Since I kind of owe you (guilty conscience over our tractor trades), I'd let you have her for $1,000." I started to say no but he quickly added "before you say anything come with me and lets go look at her." I said "ok" and finished breakfast. Then

I got in my pickup and followed Charlie to his farm right at the edge of town.

When we drove up she came right up to the fence - to me, not to Charlie. I must admit I liked that and I liked her looks. Despite her bulging tummy she was a graceful and beautiful animal. I said "I'll give $750 for her." Charlie obviously was in a "tight" for money for he said "Give me a check" - and I did. He said she should have dropped the colt a week ago and didn't think it smart to move her until the colt was born and a few weeks old. I agreed.

About four weeks later Charlie came to the ranch with the mare in the trailer and his wife holding the colt in her lap. They unloaded and I spent the day, feeding, watering, and grooming the mare and petting and grooming the colt. I called Dr. Porter and he came by and checked both animals and gave them shots. He recommended I start feeding the mare enriched food with mineral supplement - said she had been malnourished in the past. The colt was very healthy though.

Omar came up for the weekend and instantly fell in love with the little colt. He started calling him Pedro and that became his name. I named the mare Mamasita. Omar used to pet the colt while I groomed the mare. When we finished they would romp and gallop across the pasture.

After Pedro got to be a purty good sized colt, Omar suggested we start training him. He claimed to have trained several horses in the past. I thought that was a good idea and asked how we went about training Pedro. He said the first thing we would do would be to "halter break" him. We went to Bowie and bought a halter. I got a bucket of horse feed and Mamasita came right up to me and I held the bucket as she ate. I also held the new halter.

Meantime, when Pedro walked up, Omar started talking to him and petting him. Then, he grabbed Pedro around the neck and yelled -Bring the halter - quick!" I dropped the bucket and lunged toward Pedro - halter in hand. Pedro was lunging around -- doing his best to get loose and Omar was hanging on. Just as I got close and started to slip the halter over his nose - he bit Omar on the leg - Omar screamed and let go - and Pedro raced away - Mamasito right behind.

We switched our tactics. I decided to saddle Mamasita and rope Pedro. Then I would snub him to a tree and Omar would put the halter on him. I had trouble getting a saddle on Mamasita. Although she was "broke to ride," she hadn't had a saddle on her back in a long time and was, as they say, a little rank.

We finally got her saddled and I climbed aboard, lasso in hand. Each time we approached Pedro, he would move out of range of the rope. A couple of times when I made a cast at him - I missed - and Mamasita danced away. Obviously she was not a roping horse - and it was just as obvious that I was not a roper.

However, I finally got a loop over Pedro's head - and soon wished I hadn't. I forgot to wear gloves and the rope burned (and blistered) my hands. After I finally looped it around the saddle horn, Mamasita turned and the taut rope felt like it was going to cut my leg off before I finally let go of it. We gave up for the day and left Pedro trailing a rope - hoping it would "teach him a lesson."

That night we discussed a new strategy. We would outsmart them. The next morning I put horse feed in the feed trough in the corral and rigged a long rope on the gate and stretched it to our hiding place. When Mamasita and Pedro finally entered the corral we jerked the gate shut and had them trapped. I was able to get a rope on Pedro's neck and pull him to the corral fence and hold him while Omar got the halter on him. We finally got the lasso off his head and he was "haltered." But that's all - Omar tried unsuccessfully to get a lead rope tied to the halter out he couldn't. We decided to just let him get used to the halter.

That didn't work either. The next weekend Pedro was without a halter. I found it out in the pasture and had no idea how he got shed of it. (Just as I couldn't figure out how he had gotten loose of the lasso).

Pedro continued to grow on the T-Bone - and got wild as a guinea. My hip continued to deteriorate and Omar lost interest.

So, one day when a man stopped at the ranch and inquired if the horses were for sale - I decided they were and sold Mamasita and Pedro for $2,500.

I stayed out of the horse business after that.

My next door neighbor had a couple of Donkeys. They often got through the fence and grazed on the T-Bone.

<u>Cows</u>

The first herd was described in Chapter Nine. With that herd I was in a cow/calf operation. I planned to keep and raise the heifer (female) calves and to make steers out of the bull calves (castrate them) and to sell the steers when they got to be 700-800 pounds (roughly 1 year old). It is the standard age old ranching formula. However, my plans were sidetracked by a severe drought and an IRS audit when I sold everything - at a substantial loss.

I mentioned LeRoy in Chapter Nine. He was the first calf born on the T-Bone ranch. Among many lessons I learned from him were – <u>don't</u> <u>ever</u> <u>name</u> <u>cows</u>. Just put a brand on their hip and a tag (with a number on it) in their ear. An call them by the tag number from that day forward.

I had castrated LeRoy when he was a tiny calf and when he got to be around 700 pounds I decided to butcher him for the family meat. I loaded him in the trailer and hauled him to Fishers in Muenster. They grain fed him for about six weeks then butchered him, packaged and froze the meat. When they called and said the meat was ready for pickup I drove over to get it – and was I in for a shock. The meat was packed in boxes (similar to tie down file boxes) and it <u>literally</u> <u>filled</u> my pickup truck bed.

I took it back to the ranch and filled the chest type ice chest and the ice chest compartment of the refrigerator –

but hardly made a dent in it. But what to do with the rest of the meat. I called the kids and they wanted some steaks and home and Carol said to bring just a "little bit." In desperation, I called Fishers and they said there was a locker plant in Bowie that rented lockers.

I drove to Bowie and found the locker – but it was closed. It would not re-open until Monday morning. I was able to find some dry ice and iced the meat down and headed to Dallas. I delivered meat to the boys and to all the friends and relatives who wanted any. Then, on Monday morning I went by the office and gave some beef to the employees before I drove back to Bowie and rented a meat locker.

However, since LeRoy was very nearly a pet and a family member, no one in the family would eat any of the beef – except me. We ended giving most of LeRoy away and I ate on him for 2 or 3 more years.

The next spring after the drought and "Sell off" when the grass started sprouting and the birds started singing I fertilized the pastures good and decided to get back into the cattle business. Except this time, I bought a few bred limousine cows and planned to use Dale's limousine bull when the time came that I needed him.

They say "history repeats itself" and darned if it didn't. We had another drought that year and I went through another forced sale – again at a big financial loss. I was firmly convinced you couldn't make any money at ranching – even if you rustled (stole) the cows.

I'll never forget a cattle trailer parked at the auction barn loaded with old cows with their ribs showing. A crude sign on it said "Free cattle – and under that – you'll be sorry if you take one unless you got a barn full of hay."

The next year after I was so discouraged that I stayed out of the cow business (but I got Mamasita and Pedro).

But the year after I jumped back in – with a new plan. I decided to buy weaned steer calves in the spring and run them on the pasture all summer and sell them when the grass was gone. That way, my only <u>cost</u> would be the initial cost of the calves and the weight gain would be profit. Right? Brrr! Wrong!

I bought eight steer calves, kept them on grass all summer, and sold them that fail – and <u>lost</u> money (not a lot though).

It work like this.

Young calves sell for approximately $1 per pound.

Grown steers sell for approximately 70¢ per pound.

Therefore, if you buy a young steer that weighs 350 pounds it cost you $350. When you sell him at 700 pounds (at 70¢) you receive $490. You grossed $140. Deduct vet bills, branding (hired help), feed supplement, salt, minerals, and pasture fertilizer – say $200 average per head – you lost $60 per head. Not real good economics.

When they ask me "How do you get into ranching ?" My stock reply is – First – you inherit a large ranch – and a pot full of cash."

There was a story going round about an ole west Texas rancher who won $2 million in the Texas lotto. A reporter asked him "What are you going to do with all that money?" He responded "Guess I'll just keep on ranching long as the money holds out."

I also continued to add equipment. I bought an '83 Ford F-150 pickup from a widow in Garland and implements (disc, plow, auger, etc.) from an old fellow named Green in Gainesville. He and I did some "serious" horse trading.

At about the time, I went by the post office and picked up the mail. Nested among the usual junk mail was a letter from the internal revenue service, Wichita Falls, Texas. They wanted to do another tax audit on me – particularly my ranching deductions. I called them and the next week took my records to the ranch and the IRS auditor checked them out. She asked a bunch of stupid questions and it became very obvious she didn't know come here from sick em so far as ranching was concerned. The end result was this "The IRS disallowed my ranch deductions using the "hobby ranch" argument. I appealed but lost. Since I never made any profit I just decided to convent to a wild life refuge and give upon ranching. My hip had gotten so bad I could only get around with a cane or walker.

My hip got so bad that the only solution was a hip replacement. I finally had this done and was "out of action" for seven months (I think around 1995). However, after a few months I was almost back to normal and returned to my schedule – T-Bone every weekend.

At about that time Joaquin told me one Saturday that he had to quit. The company he worked for had gotten a big pipeline clearing contract and expected him to work every day – including most Sundays. I asked if he knew of anyone I could get to replace him. He said "Yes – I know a young man in Nocona who would like to job. His name is Jose and he lives with his grandparents in Nocona." He gave me his phone number and said he would tell him to expect my call – but it must be in Spanish. Jose did not speak English.

When I returned to Dallas that Sunday my wife (who is very fluent in Spanish) called the phone number. She talked to Jose and his grandparents for over an hour – occasionally asking me a questions, etc. The result was that I hired Jose and told him I would pick him up the following Saturday – which I did. He turned out to be an invaluable help to me for several years.   But he finally

moved back to Mexico.

Jose

CHAPTER 21

WHT DO YOU DO FOR FUN AROUND HERE?

Usually, the question asked by any city slicker guest, as it starts getting dark is "What do you do for fun around here."

When I tell them I love to sit on the porch and listen to the coyotes howl; then go to bed and read a good book they look at me like I was crazy – or maybe just weird. They usually prod further and I explain – "If you mean movies, bars, and other man made foolishness – you left most of that in the city. The nearest theater is 70 miles away in Decatur. And if you want to go to a beer joint – there is club 59 outside Montague, the VFW hall in Bowie, and the Stardust in Lindsey – either one of which could get your tail whipped in a New York minute.

Also, at the Stardust you can do a little really belly rubbing two stepping with the local lassies. I explained that most of the local entertainment is sporadic or seasonal – not an every night or every weekend thing. They want details so I continue-

(1) The Saint Jo Opry – this is a takeoff of the grand ole Opry and is presented in the high school auditorium in Saint Jo on the second Saturday of each month. The entertainers are local musicians along with area guest entertainers. Most of the music is country and western. It's a lot of fun and cheap - $2.

(2) Watermelon fest – Forestburg – once a year (sept)

(3) German fest – Muenster – once a year (April)

(4) Chicken and bread days – Bowie (Aug)

(5) 4th of July – everywhere

(6) Rodeo's – everywhere

(7) High school sports – everywhere

(8) Winstar Casino – Oklahoma (just across the border)

All of the fests are similar – streets roped off, live music, games, food and drink – big crowds. All the local towns have rodeo arenas – most rodeo's are amateurs – some ranch vs. ranch completion.

Some of the local towns have fireworks shows on July 4th – but the best show was at the T-Bone.

And there are two excellent restaurant close:

*Prime cut steak house (Montague)

*Times Forgotten (Nocona)

The July 4th barbecue and fireworks show has become a tradition at the T-Bone ranch. Friends and family come up to feast on the barbecue, sitting in the shade, and drink beer, and watch the fireworks show

that Michael, Kenneth, and I put on after it gets dark.

The standard menu I usually prepare is:

Barbecue meats:

　*Ribs
　*Turkey
　*Brisket
　*Chicken
Potatoe salad
Pinto beans
Cole slaw
Sliced tomatoes
Corn on the cob
Cokes and/or cold beer
Followed by –
　*Cold watermelon
　*Homemade ice cream

Yummy, my mouth waters just writing about it.

There is also bingo across in Oklahoma at the Indian

reservations.　Hamilton and I went up there one

Saturday night and there must have been 300 people

packed in the bingo parlor. They haul them in by the bus load from the DFW area.

And finally, the Winstar Casino just across the Red River from Gainesville has expanded to the point it nearly (but not quite) compares to Las Vegas.

Almost forgot – there is a winery and pizza place north of Saint Jo at Spanish fort. (Arche winery and Ancient Ovens).

And I'm sure there other things available if you went looking for them. Me, I'll stick to reading. Over the years I have accumulated quite a liberty – mostly westerns from yard sales, 2nd Monday, etc. My favorite books are western fiction and my favorite authors are:

* Louis Liamour * Zane Grey * J.T. Edson

*Ralph Compton * J. Frank Dobie * Max Brand

* T.V. Olsen

I have also accumulated a large collection of movies

- John Wayne westerns and classics, including:

*Gone With The Wind *Lawrence of Arabia

*Giant   *Lonesome Dove *Out of Africa

*Casablanca *African Queen *Benny Hill Comedies

*Alamo

CHAPTER 22

EXPANSION

When my mother died I inherited some money. I gave most of it to the kids and took the rest to buy another piece of land that joined the T-Bone on the east side. The piece of land I bought was across the creek and it was solid woods, brush and vines.

The creek banks were sheer drop offs - about 40 feet deep. You could not cross to get to the added land. Therefore, it was almost useless. Unless a bridge was built to connect it.

I decided to try to clear it by selling the timber. I ran an ad in the shopper and two or three locals came by and looked at it - but weren't interested in my terms. Matter of fact, they wanted me to pay them to cut the trees - then give them the trees.

Finally, a man from Henrietta showed up who was in the firewood business - big time. He offered to cut the trees, ground level, burn the limbs and brush, and pay $20 per cord for all the wood he cut. He gave references and I checked him out and made a deal with him.

Then I bought some bright orange colored ribbon and marked all the trees he couldn't cut and he went to work. He ended by cutting only the trees on the west side of the creek - the easy side - but never got across to the jungle. One weekend when I got to the ranch there was a check on the door and a note that said "I'm through."

The ranch remained "status quo" until we started Freeman Lake a couple of years later.

CHAPTER 23

FREEMAN LAKE

After we bought the additional acreage I decided the best solution for the land usage would be to dam the creek and create a small lake. The creek was deep enough that it would not require much digging for the lake itself - only to build the dam. The resultant lake would be long and narrow with a fork in it and would back up to the gravel road along the front of the ranch. I had a contractor out of Bowie come out and give me an estimate for the dam I envisioned and he bid $12,000.

A few weekends later, Howard came up for a visit and I showed him what I planned to do. He advised against it - said I would not be  satisfied with a small narrow lake and that it would over - flow the spillway every time it rained and that a really hard rain might cause it to collapse the dam.

Instead, he said he would build a "real" lake for us and it would only  cost his "out of pocket" costs. He admitted that we had done a lot for him and he was in our debt. (By then he had his new business - up and running in Palestine, Texas and was starting to make a nice profit.) So, I took him at his word and said "Ok - let's do it." Thus began a year long ordeal that taxed my patience to the limit and almost brought an end to our friendship.)

The next weekend when I got to the ranch there was was a huge bulldozer parked by the old shack. It was a caterpillar D-8 (I think the largest made). Later that morning, Howard and his Dozier operator, William, arrived in a big Mack truck hauling a Caterpillar 955 loader. The D-8 wouldn't run so all weekend was spent taking it apart and chasing all over north Texas - looking for parts. (there was a Caterpillar dealer in Wichita Falls(open till noon Saturday) and a used heavy equipment dealer in Nocona (sometimes open on Saturday - sometimes not) plus various auto parts houses.) Howard did knock down a few trees and expand the pond a little with the 955 but William never got the D-8 running. Howard took the dirt he dug from the pond and started a road base for the road that ran from the front gate to the back of the property.

Sunday afternoon, they loaded the 955 on the trailer but before they left Howard said "You owe me $10,000." I said "What for?" He said "That's what I paid for that D-8." (he had  bought the old D-8 from someone in Sulphur Springs for $10,000 - to Howard, that was "out of pocket" expense). I gave him the $10,000 and should have for seen what was ahead - but didn't.

They were already there the next weekend when I got there (Friday late afternoon). I rigged up a light and William worked  on the D-8 until late into the night - they had brought parts from the cat dealer in Tyler). I have always been a believer in having the right tool to do a job. Therefore, over the years I have accumulated a shop full of good tools. William said "There are more tools in the T-Bone shop than any auto garage in Palestine. Howard and I watched T.V. while William worked on the D-8. He finally quit around midnight and we went to bed.

I woke up around 5 a.m. and heard the D-8 chug - chugging in the distance. I made a pot of coffee and Howard got up. We took our coffee and a cup for

William and drove down to where he was working. He had already cleared some of the woods and had two big piles of trees - roots and all. He stopped and we drank coffee and Howard explained the plan. First they had to clear out the woods before he could "shoot" the dam and lake and stake it out. Made sense. Then he told me what they needed - diesel fuel, Delo oil, hydraulic oil, starter fluid, bottled water, ice, cokes. They had brought a 200 gallon fuel trailer - in bad shape - especially the tires.

I saw right away what my job was going to be - procurer, delivery boy, and cook. I told them breakfast would be ready in 45 minutes so I went back to the trailer and fixed sausage, eggs, biscuits and gravy. They showed up on time and we ate. After breakfast, Howard got on the 955 and continued his project. And William got back on the D-8 and continued knocking down trees.

I hooked up the fuel trailer, loaded a couple of tires I had taken off the Tahoe when I bought new tires, and headed for Bowie. I went to a service station that "specialized" in tires and tire repair and they changed the tires on the fuel trailer. Then I took it to a welding shop and they welded some broken

places. Next I went by the Conoco Distributor and got most of the "supplies," then by Levels Super Market for the cokes, ice, and water - then back to the T-Bone.

When I arrived I found Howard and William at the trailer – watching T.V. The D-8 had quit running again. William thought he knew what was wrong. Howard called the Cat dealer in Wichita Falls and they had the parts that William needed. They agreed to stay a little past 12 and wait for

us. We jumped in the Tahoe (after unhitching the fuel trailer and unloading the rest of the stuff) and headed for Wichita Falls – 70 miles away. It was about 10:50 a.m. We drove purty fast and rolled into the cat parking lot at 12:15 and went inside. They had the parts ready – along with the ticket - $340 (and you know who paid).

We ate lunch and headed back to the T-Bone. The rest of the afternoon was spent – working on the D-8. William finally got it running again and worked till dark. They worked till noon on Sunday and headed back to Palestine. They had cleared enough of the trees and brush that Howard said he would bring his instruments and stake out the project the next weekend.

The following weekend the "real" work began. Howard  "shot" the dam and lake and William drove red tipped stakes around what was to be the shoreline. It was to be much larger than I had envisioned. I watched as they cranked up both machines and started moving dirt. First they removed the overburden (top layer) on the hill on the west bank until they got down to the clay. Next they pushed dirt over the bank and built a ramp to the bottom of the gully. Then they started pushing clay into the gulley, creating the core of the dam. Clearly Howard, an engineer, knew what he was doing. (he had built 4 large lakes on his own ranch plus several others for customers) William was learning fast.

Things seemed to be going too good – and they changed before the day was over. A drive wheel on the D-8 broke. They were able to drag it out of the creek with the 955. We called Nocona and they had a used wheel which we went and got - $350. William spent the rest of Saturday and most of Sunday fixing the D-8. They left at noon on Sunday.

The next several weekends were about the same. Howard would operate the 955 and William the D-8. Joaquin continued to saw the downed trees into firewood and Santiago came a few Saturdays to help him. I continued to chase parts, cook, and haul fuel.

I don't remember a single weekend that the D-8 did not break down and quit. Most of the problems were either in the fuel system or the hydraulic systems. It leaked like a sieve. However, sometimes something really big broke – the cables that lifted the blade, the breaks, the starter, etc. even though the D-8 was fundamentally a sound machine – it had not been taken care of and had sat idle for a couple of years before Howard bought it.

Finally the day came when William just could not fix it. Howard concluded it had to go to a Caterpillar dealer for a complete front to back overhaul. So they got it loaded - on the trailer and hauled it to Wichita Falls and left it. He and William decided to "Take a break" until the D-8 was fixed.

About a month passed and Howard called and said the D-8 was ready. He asked me to meet them at the Cat dealer in Wichita Falls at 3:00 p.m. on Friday and by the way –

bring a check for $16,000. He had me over the barrel –
and knew it. If I didn't pay the project would be
abandoned and would be one big mess. I didn't have that
much cash on hand and had to borrow from Michael to
cover the check.

I met them and they loaded the D-8. It had been
repainted and had new decals. Looked like a new
bulldozer. Howard kind of joked about me covering the
"out o pocket" costs and I seethed. (It now was obvious
what he had done – gotten a D-8 bulldozer now worth at
least $50,000 for his and William labor – I had paid for
it.)

However, things went a lot smoother now that the D-8 was fixed and they moved one helluva lot of dirt. The dam and lake were taking shape, Joaquin finished cutting and we got the limbs burned. In the process of burning the brush piles, we cooked about a dozen copperhead snakes. They would slither out of the brush pile and Joaquin or I would whack them with a shovel and toss them back into the fire. There was so much dirt in the piles that they did not burn out completely. I left them as is figuring whatever wood and roots were left would rot I in a few years and I could level them with my tractor and blade.

Before the lake was completed they brought a large track hoe and used it to "shape" the banks so there were no sheer drop offs. I also had a man from Bowie bring several loads of gravel which Howard spread on the ranch roads.

Toward the end of the project, things were much more relaxed and we started going out for most of our meals. We would sleep later and quit earlier. I built a boat dock. The pressure was off. Finally, the lake was completed.

Winter came and passed and with the arrival of spring came the heavy rains. One weekend when I arrived at the ranch – the lake was full of water and looked great. Jose came out to help me start a new project and he and I got a barrel I had cut in half and the fishing pole and went down to the pond and caught dozens of fish – mostly catfish but also perch and bass and transplanted them to the new lake. A couple of weekends later I bought minnows, perch and bass fingerlings and put them into the lake also. Ever since I've fed the fish ever weekend and they have grown – a lot.

Later in the spring I got a call from Howard. He asked if he and William could come up the next weekend and see the lake. I said "sure". That was the first contact with him since the lake

was completed.

That weekend they showed up. They were very proud of the lake – as was I. I said "Howard, I appreciate what you have done and have named the lake. "Freeman Lake."

In retrospect, the lake project was a good deal for all of us. Howard got his bulldozer (which he still owns and uses everyday), William learned how to build a lake (and got paid doing so – by Howard), and we got the ranch cleared up and Freeman Lake built (which increased the

value of the T-Bone).

CHAPTER 24

CHESTER

Because of the remote locations of the ranch and because of my bad habit of tossing table scraps out the back door – stray dogs and cats were always showing up at the T-Bone. The neighbors dogs always came over for a visit when they knew I was at the T-Bone.

Once when I was sitting on the porch I heard dogs (puppies actually) whining and crying. The noise was coming from the direction of the front gate. Curiosity got the best of me so I walked to the front gate. A cardboard box was sitting in the weeds by the road it contained six pitiful little black puppies. They were covered with filth and flea's and nearly starved.

I went back and got the pickup and came and got there and took them to the trailer. I made some oatmeal and poured canned milk in it and fed them. Then I gave them a bath and drowned most of the flea's. After I dried them off, they really came alive and were extremely playful and feisty.

Late that day, I drove to town and got flee spray and puppy chow. But I couldn't figure out what to do with them. I needed to get back to Dallas. I called Dale and the Hamptons – neither wanted them.

So, I got a large cardboard box and an old blanket and made them a dog house. I left them a big pan of food and a pan of water and headed for Dallas. I planned to come back to the ranch by the end of the week – hopefully Thursday – to check on them and find them a new home.

However, when I returned to the ranch on Thursday afternoon – the puppies were gone – as was most of the food and water. I searched everywhere for them but they had disappeared without a trace. To this day I have no idea what happened to those little guys.

The next animal that showed up was a cat. He (or she) stayed around the barn and was wild – I never was able to touch him. I left cat food out for him (her) and it could come during the night and eat it and I would see it from time to time – but he remained basically – wild. I finally quit seeing it and it's disappearance is also a mystery.

When Howard and William were building the lake a beautiful blue heeler (dog) with those strange white eyes showed up We fed him and he really took up with

William. When we left that weekend I left a big pan of food and a bucket of water for him.

Lo and behold – when we arrived at the ranch the next weekend the blue heeler was there – waiting for us. He had scratched out a bed under the porch. The food had been eaten. Howard had brought his dog, a large female Rottweiler named bear and she went to meet the blue heeler and I went inside and got dog food and another pan and put it out – both dogs ate and I filled the water bucket for them.

This scene was repeated for the next 3 weekends. Finally, William said to me "Do you mind if I take that dog back to Palestine?" I said "Not at all – take him." He did.

Several months passed and no more "strays" appeared. Then in the early summer of 2003, Howard and William had come up to spend the weekend. William was fixing the riding lawn mower and Howard and I were sitting in the shade –supervising – when this half grown pup walked up. At first he was shy and stand offish but when we talked to him he wagged his tail and came to me and I petted him. He was full of fleas and ticks and half starved. His ribs were showing. His marking appeared that he was a mix between a beagle and pointer (bird dog)

I went to the trailer and got a pan of dog food and opened a can of pet milk and poured in it. He wolfed that down instantly – and was still hungry. So I went back inside and rummaged through the freezer and found a container of beef stew which I put in the microwave. When it was ready I fed him the stew and he wolfed it down too – but it filled him. His tummy was bulging.

Next I gave him a bath and got rid of most of the flea's and then I pulled off the ticks and smashed them. I put an old blanket on the porch and he curled up on it and slept all afternoon.

That night when we went to Bowie to eat I stopped by Levels Supermarket and got flea powder, a flea collar, a toy, and a sack of Purina puppy chow. The pup was waiting for us when we returned so I poured him a bowl of puppy chow put on the flea collar, and dusted him with the powder. We sat on the porch for awhile, talked, and took turns petting the pup. He was white with black spots – and some brown. He looked just like "snoopy" from the comic strip. We concluded that he was a beagle/bird dog mix and about 6 months old. (The vet later reached the same conclusion). I think someone had hauled him to the country and "dropped him." (Probably a bird hunter whose bird dog has an illicit affair with the neighbors beagle).

The next morning I fed him again and gave him a can of milk - and he followed us around the ranch all day. That night we went to town to eat and I brought back a doggie bag containing a part of a steak I couldn't eat, plus bones, and the remains of baked potatoes. He devoured them – then played with the Styrofoam box. I got out his toy – a rubber dumbbell with a whistle and William started teaching him to retrieve it.

Sunday, before we left, I filled all the available pans I could find with puppy chow and filled a bucket of water and left them on the porch. He followed us to the front gate and I had to throw rocks at him to chase him back.

But the next weekend when I entered the front gate and drove toward the trailer – he ran out to meet me. I took him to the vet for his shots, worming, and anti flea treatment. The girl at the office filled out a form for him and asked his name. On the spur of the moment I said "Chester A. Arthur." She giggled and wrote it down. (I had been listening to the car radio and a question had been asked on a call in show – "who was the 21st President of the USA?" Several callers missed it but finally someone called in with the correct answer – Chester A. Arthur – and that's how Chester got named).

I bought a dog house for him and fixed a feed trough with a roof which is nailed to the porch. The biggest fault he has is that he drags everything he can get a hold on out into the yard to play with it. I left the trailer door open once and he went in and got my boots and shoes.

Once when I was working on something he got the hammer and a screwdriver. He has drug his blanket out in the yard many times. I'm constantly picking up stuff he drags into the yard – limbs, cans, paper, etc. etc. I scold him and plan to whack him if I ever catch him in the act. Or best yet, maybe he will grown out of it.

He was a lot of company for me. I drove the tractor all over the ranch and he ran along – exploring all the strange smells. He chases deer, rabbits, squirrels,. etc. and frantically digs for field mice. I've watched him catch grass hoppers, lizards, and small frogs at the pond – and eat them. He must have survived in that manner before he came to the T-Bone.

Chester did not run like a normal dog. He leaped like a deer. He had chased them so much he learned to leap like them.

When Caro began coming to the ranch she "adopted" Chester and took him to Dallas and he spent the rest of his life there. He got sick in 2004 and she took him to the vet. They diagnosed his problem as "heart worms" and their treatment killed him. He now rests in the T-Bone pet cemetery.

CHAPTER 25

THE "NEW" HACIENDA

Caro would come to the ranch on July 4th for the annual barbecue and other rare occasions but would not spend the night in the old house trailer. I knew I must get better living accommodations if ever I expected my bride to spend the night at the T-Bone.

One weekend in 2007 when I sat down to read the mail (which I picked up at the post office box in Saint Jo) the following ad in the Shopper (Montague County Paper) caught my eye.

Huge Bargain - 14 X 80 house trailer - couple must sell - make an offer.

I called the phone number listed and talked to the owner. The house trailer was located just outside Forestburg so I decided to go look at it.

The trailer was practically new. It had 3 bedrooms, a large den or living room, kitchen and dining room, and two full baths. It was in great shape - just what I needed. The owner had been injured at work and

was disabled. He owned a small ranch outside Forestburg and he and his wife had started building their dream home on their ranch before his injury. They had 3 children and lived in a rent house in Forestburg.

In his "settlement" with his employer, he was given this trailer which was set up on his ranch so he would be close to the house he was building. He could still do "light" work and his wife helped him. Their new house was nearly complete but they had run out of money and desperately needed cash to finish some inside work - carpeting, cabinets, painting, etc.

After some horse trading, we finally made a deal. I paid them cash for the trailer and agreed they could continue living in it until they were able to move into their new house - with a 60 day limit.

Next I got William to haul off the old trailer and he, Jose and I got the needed measurements from the new trailer and staked out the set up area for it. I decided to set it up perpendicular to where the old trailer had been so we could use the septic tank already in place. We then dug the ditches for the water lines and sewer and I hired a local plumber to install the water and sewer lines.

In about 45 days the people called and said they were moved and the trailer was ready. I hired movers to pick up the trailer and bring  it to the T-Bone. We knew it was too large to make it through the front gate so we took down about 50 feet of the front fence. However, it rained a couple of days before they delivered the trailer and they got stuck in the mud at the gap in the gene. Fortunately, our new neighbor (who had bought Dale's place) had a D-5 bulldozer and when he saw what had happened he came over on his bulldozer, chained to the truck - and pulled them to dry ground. They maneuvered the trailer to the set up, unhitched it, and set it up level. The water lines and sewer fit perfectly. The next step was getting the plumber and electrician out to get it hooked up.

Caro came out the next weekend and brought Annabelle, who did "handyman" work for us in Dallas. Caro insisted that we add a glassed in front porch and a solid underpinning. I contracted with Annabelle to build the porch and add a concrete block foundation (and re-build the pump house.)

Annabelle brought Leo and 5 other Mexicans out the next week to start the project(s). I had purchased the materials from Community Lumber in Muenster and it had been delivered and was ready when the crew arrived. They brought tents and camping equipment and set up their camp down by the lake.

First, we moved the furniture that had been stored in the old shack into the new trailer and I hired a delivery service to haul furniture

and a refrigerator from Dallas to the new trailer - it was now habitable so Caro, Annabelle, and I stayed in the new trailer while the building took place. The air conditioner wasn't doing a good job so I bought a new 4 ton Trane that did an excellent job. I also had the Direct TV crew from Jacksboro come out and move the satellite dish and bought a large used Emerson TV from Annabelle - all the comforts of home.

Everyone was complaining about the water (smell, taste, etc.) - so I next had a water treatment system installed.

The construction was completed and we had a barbecue and fish fry to celebrate - also homemade ice cream. I let  Leo and his crew fish in the lake and they caught a bunch of fish.

They were in no hurry to return to Dallas - the T-Bone had grown on them.

Annabelle saw a baby deer stand up in the front pasture. She, Leo and his crew surrounded it and captured it and brought it to the trailer. It was about a week old and Annabelle named it Princess. She and Caro took turns holding it like a baby. It was nearly starved so I had to drive to Bowie and get a baby bottle and formula - it drank  all I brought. They insisted we take it back to Dallas - which we did. When they handed it to me to hold - I renamed it <u>Prince</u>. It was a he. I called the Texas Game and Fish and they told me to take it to a lady in Athens who took care of orphaned animals. I called her and she told me to bring the little deer right over. So Caro, Prince, and I made the trip to Athens. I talked to her on my cell phone and got directions to her place called "Deer Heaven". She had a pen containing about 6 small deer (all females) and put Prince in with the girls. He seemed happy. I also gave her a sizeable contribution. I kept in touch with her and learned that Prince survived and grew up and now resides at a girl scout camp near Palestine.

CHAPTER 26

THE BARNETT SHALE AND WIND GENERATORS

As I mentioned in Chapter 11, the economy in Montague County was bad - very bad. In fact, it was one of the poorest counties in the entire state of Texas. However, that changed in about 2008 when it was discovered that the Barnett Shale formation was in a layer of stratus about 8,000 feet below the surface - practically throughout the county. More precisely, oil companies had figured out how to extract the natural gas and hydrocarbons from the shale formation by a process of horizontal drilling and next fracturing the formation to allow the gas to escape.

The first wave of the gas play were the land men who invaded the county to sign up leases. When I purchased the property I only got the surface rights. The mineral rights were owned by about 60 ancestors of the original owner (an Italian farmer). I tried at that time to buy the mineral rights but was not successful - these 60 folks we're scattered all over the world. (incidentally - I think the law should be changed so that mineral rights stay with surface rights - it doesn't make sense to separate them.)

I don't know how many land men stopped by the ranch to get a lease signed - pipeline easement, seismic contract, etc. There were many. (the ones too lazy to go by the court house and check).

Next came the Seismic crews. I would not allow them to "shoot" Seismic on the property although I found evidence where they did anyway when I wasn't there.

The next wave were the pipeline layers who wanted to lay a pipeline the entire east/west length of the property. I would not allow this either.

In other words - I wanted all of them to stay the heck off the T-Bone ranch and leave us alone.

Next came the drilling crews who started drilling wells all over the county. An above surface water line was strung across the front of the property and stayed there for months. Three wells were drilled on the Truman Weed property to my west - just across the fence. I am sure they did directional drilling right under the T-Bone.

Next construction crews came in are built gas processing plants, pumping station, gas gathering lines, etc.

It seems that a huge truck passes in front of the ranch every 10 minutes raising a cloud of dust and tearing heck out of the road.

For people like me, all this oil and gas activity has been a huge <u>negative</u>. but for the mineral interest owners, they brought manna from heaven and on behalf of the oil companies, I must credit them with a huge economic stimulus to the local economy. They provided many jobs for folks who were hurting.

In addition to the inconvenience and aggravation to humans, all this activity has a very noticeable effect on the wild life. Deer, in particular, move deeper into the woods and rarely showed themselves during daylight hours.

At this same time of the intense oil and gas activity, they were also building wind driven electricity generators north - and east of Saint Jo. Progress? Maybe.

The point is - all this progress has been <u>detrimental</u> to the peace and quiet of the T-Bone ranch. It just isn't the same.

CHAPTER 27

MORE "TOYS"

On another occasion (probably in 2008) I was reading the "Shopper" again and saw an ad - 4 wheeler - for sale or trade - phone xxx-xxxx.

I had been think of getting an ATV (4 wheeler) for a few years but didn't think they were worth the price. (upward of $10,000 for the ATV trucks which I wanted). I thought, may as well check this out. I called and made arrangements to go look at the 4 wheeler. It was located near Alvord (about 30 miles west). When I got there the place was located out in a wooded area off a FM road and there were junk pickup everywhere you looked. It was a used truck "scavenger" yard.

The owner was a beady eyed roly poly man who was talking to a customer when I drove up in my Chevy Cheyenne (3/4 ton pickup). We visited for a few minutes and he pulled out his cell phone and called his house which sat back in the woods. In a few minutes we heard the put - putting of the 4 wheeler and a young man rode up on a bright red Honda 4 wheeler. It looked and was practically new. I liked it and we started the "horse trade."

His cash (asking) price was almost double my offer - if was obvious we could never bridge the gap. He next wanted to swap even for my Chevrolet pickup. I would not even consider a swap unless he threw in a considerable amount of "boot".

We haggled a while and another "customer" showed up. To look at the Honda. They negotiated a while out of earshot and the "customer" got in his car and drove off. While they were bickering I had a brilliant idea - trade my Ford pickup for the Honda.

When he came back he told me he thought that feller that just left was going to buy the Honda - he had to go home and see if his wife would loan him the money first. I figured that might not be exactly true so I made him the offer - my '82 Ford pickup for the Honda ATV - even swap. He thought about it and said "Bring the Ford here and let me check it out - maybe we can then work out a trade."

I really wasn't sure the old Ford could make the trip so I said "I've got a better idea" load the Honda in this truck (my Chevy); hop in and I'll take you to my ranch and you can check out the Ford pickup all you like - if it suits you. I'll sign the title and hand you the keys and you can drive it back. He hesitated, then said "Junior, I've got a customer coming by in a few minutes - what is your schedule?" Junior said "Nothing this morning". The man said "Go with this feller and check out his Ford - then call me." We loaded the Honda and Junior got in - in about 45 minutes we pulled into the T-Bone.

The old Ford had not been used in quite a while and wouldn't start - I got the jumper cables and it fired up. Junior spent about 30 minutes checking it out and test driving it. Then I observed him on his cell phone - obviously  talking to his dad. He got out of the Ford and came over to me and said "Did you know that the reverse doesn't work on the Ford?" I said "Yes, and I told your dad about it before we left your place. (I had really down played the old Ford when I described it to the old man - knowing it was in better shape than I described it to him). Junior said "Dad said he would trade for $1,000 boot." I said "No boot - hop in and I'll take you home." He climbed in and we headed toward the front gate. When we got to the gate he said "Stop here for a minute".

I stopped and he pulled out his cell phone and made a call. I couldn't hear what dad said but Junior said. (1) he won't give no boot. (2) Yes sir (3) yes sir (4) no sir (5) it's a purty good looking old Ford - cowboy blue and grey, grill guard, tool box, very good mud grip tires (6) yes sir, I would trade (7) ok, I'll be home in about 45 minutes in a Ford pickup. He put the phone in his pocket and said "turn around - we got a deal."

We drove back to the house, unloaded the Honda, I got the title and signed it - and he drove off in the Ford. I was saddened to see it leave - it had been a good one.

However, after he left and I tried to ride the Honda I wasn't so sure I had made a good trade. It had a "pull" starter and was hard to start and it was extremely painful for me to get a straddle of it - same problem I had climbing on a horse. Oh well, my sons and granddaughters would enjoy it - it would really scoot across the pasture.

The Honda did not solve my problem - that is, a mode of transportation for getting around the ranch - other than the Chevy pickup or Ford tractor.

The next time that William visited he tinkered with the Honda some and put in new spark plugs and got it fixed so it was easier to start. However, he couldn't fix my straddling problem. He told me I needed something easier to get in and out of and knew just the thing.

A couple of months later William came up and was grinning from ear to ear. he had me come out to his pickup and look at my "Christmas present" - a golf cart. He unloaded it and we rode around on it a while. It was a vast improvement over hobbling around with my walker.

My wife came up a couple of weeks later and really made fun of it. It was pretty beat up and battered - looked like it had hit a few trees or posts. Further, the batteries were about shot. A golf cart store had recently opened on Hwy 62 just outside Gainesville. I got Annabelle to help load the beat up golf cart into the Chevy pickup and took it to Gainesville to the new shop.

I asked for an estimate for the body repair and for new batteries and tires. It was about $2,500 as I recall. I decided to try somewhere else - maybe Dallas - and got in my truck to leave. As I started up the man yelled at me "would you consider a trade? I turned off the engine and said "maybe - what have you got in mind?" He said "Wait here just a minute and let me go get Dave, the owner." I said "Ok".

In a couple of minutes he returned with Dave and we started "horse trading". Dave said he had just bought 50 Yamaha's at auction and at a good price.   They had started arriving (from a country club in Miami, Florida) and he was just finishing running the first batch through his shop, putting new batteries in them, replacing tires when necessary, etc. He offered to swap for $2,000 boot. I said "I'm interested - bring one out so I can examine it." He yelled at the salesman I had talked to earlier and in a minute he drove one out for my inspection. He showed me the manufacture plate that bore out his claim they were <u>one</u> year old. This on looked <u>new</u> and the batteries were no doubt new.

I asked "will you take a check?" He asked "Have you got identification with you" I showed him my driver's license and gave him my business card. He said "deal". We went into his office where his secretary took care of the paper work and the salesman loaded my "new" Yamaha. I just love it. Now I can ride instead of hobble around the place.

CHAPTER 28

CATS, CATS, AND MORE CATS

One spring day (in 2008 I think) I was piddling around in my shop (the old shack) and I kept hearing very faint meow, meows. I could not locate the source of the meows until I stepped outside and sat down to listen and watch.

In a few minutes a couple of tiny kitten heads appeared

peeping out from under the old shack. I went to Nocona and bought milk and cat food. I put a pan of milk and another of cat food by the hole. The kittens would not come out as long as I was around. However, when I went to the house for a while and returned - the pans were empty.

Later I built a small house for them and put it on the back porch. As the kittens grew and started eating solid food, they came to the porch with mama cat for chow.

Out of that first batch of wild cats (mama and six kittens), three of the kittens survived and one of the survivors had a litter of five in 2011. I finally was able to catch one in a live trap and take her to the vet in Saint Jo and get her spayed . As I write this, the mama and two kittens are still on the ranch. They are wild as March hares and have not been domesticated. However, when I take the feed (canned cat food) out for them they don't run from me anymore.

Caro and Anabell came up one weekend and Anabell captured one litter of five kittens and took them back to

Dallas. Caro took them to the vet who gave them shots, etc. She finally was able to get the SPCA to take 3 of them - but she kept two for the granddaughter to play with. Olivia named them Baby and Cutsie Violet. They are near grown and have become a "problem".

CHAPTER 29

DRY AS A POPCORN FART

There is absolutely no question that weather patterns change over time. During the early years (1980's and 1990's), there were storms every spring and many tornados along the Red River. It always got hot in the summer and we had 10-20 days of 100° or greater. We normally got enough rain year round so that we had grass in the pastures from April through September. In addition, you could count on two cutting of hay.

In 2011, we had the other extreme - hot and dry. It got hot in May and hotter thereafter - 69 days of temperatures in excess of 100° and practically no rain. By July the grass was brown and by September the tank and lake had dried up. How hot was it? You may ask.

Well sir, it was hotter than a set of jumper cables at a Juneteenth 4th of July picnic. The coons and cranes had a feast on all the fish that were killed - literally hundreds of them. It was a sad situation.

There were grass fires all over Texas and many houses burned. The damage was in the millions. But, like they say in Texas. If you don't like the weather just hang around a day or two - it will change. Even though most of the state is experiencing several droughts - it may be flooding next year.

We were fortunate in that we located a replacement for Jose. One weekend in May of 2011, Caro and I stopped at the produce stand in Montague that was owned and operated by a Mexican family from Nocona. Caro asked (in Spanish) if they knew of anyone who would be interested in part-time ranch work. Luck was with us.

The owner said "Yes, her brother was looking for work but he was in poor health and could not do anything involving heavy lifting." We left directions to the T-Bone and asked if she would send him out to talk to us."

And that is how we found Pedro. I hired him to come by twice a week - Wednesday and Saturday to water the fruit and nut trees and shrubs and to feed the cats. He has saved nearly all the orchard - I'm sure with him we would have lost all of them - probably 50 or more. And of course, it was a godsend for Pedro - he couldn't find a better job for his condition.

By the way, it finally rained in early October (2011) - almost 6 inches.

CHAPTER 30

THE FUTURE

My hip has gotten so bad that I now have trouble just walking - without a cane I am immobile. However, I am still able to drive the tractor and riding lawn mower. I get around on the ranch in my golf cart.

My favorite "Activity" is sitting on the back porch and watching the birds, hummingbirds, cats, and wildlife. There is a deer feeder across the fence and bird feeders and hummingbird feeder by the corner of the back porch.

I still get up early (around 5:00 a.m.), fix a pot of coffee, and go sit on the porch, feed the cats, and drink coffee, watch and listen, until after daylight. I do the same just before dark. At these times I am totally relaxed and enjoying every moment.

Who knows what the future holds? I certainly don't.

There have been so many changes in my lifetime to absolutely boggle the - mind; some good and some bad.

Despite our improved standards of living and the tremendous advancements in technology, I am convinced that man has an ingrown desire (even need) to "return to the land." I've often said "my generation struggled to get out of the sticks and get to the bright lights of the city - then spent the rest of their lives trying to figure out a way to get back to the sticks".

Besides, when I started my weekend commutes to the T-Bone (appx. 75 miles from our home in Dallas) n 1984 - it took about 1 1/2 hours - today (2012) - it takes 2 1/2 to 3 hours. And it now takes about an hour just to get out of Dallas. What a congested concrete jungle it has become.

The T-Bone ranch has given me much pleasure, and, I think, added years to my life. It is indescribably peaceful and relaxing.

The End

BOOKS WRITTEN BY
BILL R. THOMAS

Title	Brief Description
1) A Summer on Piney Creek	A Summer Spent with Friend Living in a Cave on Piney Creek (Kentucky)
2) Hickory Fired Tobacco, Moonshine Whiskey, Beautiful Horses, and Fast Women	Kentucky Based Short Stories
3) Bill T's Texas Bob Tales	Texas Based Short Stories
4) I Smell Smoke	Authors Experience as B-47 Crew Member in Strategic Air Command
5) My Most Memorable Adventures - One Hunting and One Fishing	Hunting Trip in Mexico and Fishing Trip in Alaska
6) The Accumulated Wisdom of the Bugscuffle Domino, Whittle and Spit Club	Philosophy and Wisdom Gained Over a Colorful Lifetime
7) The T-Bone Ranch	Developing a Cattle Ranch in Montague County, Texas
8) A Wild Shot In The Dark	Autobiography - Birth Through Air Force
9) The Debits Are On The Left, The Credits Are By The Window	Autobiography - Air Force to Present

Books may be purchased at - Lulu.com (Bill's Books)

www.ingramcontent.com/pod-product-compliance
Lightning Source LLC
LaVergne TN
LVHW011343080426
835511LV00005B/114